Cr
Coach & I
Handbook

Written by
Paul Fawcett M Phil FCIT

Edited by
Colin Clark AMInstTA

CRONER PUBLICATIONS LIMITED

Croner House, London Road,
Kingston upon Thames, Surrey KT2 6SR

Telephone 081-547 3333

Croner's Coach & Bus Driver's Handbook

First Edition 1987
Second Edition 1989
Third Edition 1993

© Copyright Croner Publications Ltd
ISBN 1 85524 231 1

All rights reserved. No part of this publication may be reproduced, stored in a retrieval system or transmitted in any form or by any means, electronic, mechanical, photocopying, recording, or otherwise, without the prior permission of Croner Publications Ltd

CONTENTS

INTRODUCTION

OPERATORS' LICENCES

CAR SHARING	1
GROUP HIRE	1
TYPES OF LICENCE	2
Standard licences	3
Restricted licences	3
Special restricted licences	4
Permits	4
Community Bus permits	4

RUNNING A LOCAL SERVICE

EFFECTS OF DE-REGULATION	6
No monopoly	6
Reaction to competition	6
Powers of Traffic Commissioners	6
Drivers' behaviour on the road	6
LOCAL SERVICES	6
London local service licences	7
Timings	7
Retiming of school journeys	7
Duplication	8
Traffic regulation conditions	8
Bus stations and bus stops	8
Hail and ride	9
Faretables, timetables and destination notices	9
Taxis	9
Fuel tax rebates	10
COMPETITION LAW	10
TENDERED SERVICES	10
CONCESSIONARY FARES	11
COMMUNITY TRANSPORT	11
SCHEDULES AND DUTIES	11
The service timetable	12
The bus running board	14

CREW ALLOCATION	18
Daily limits	18
Weekly limits	19
Driving duties	19
Overtime	19
Types of duty	20
THE DEPOT'S DAILY DUTY ROTA	21
Size of the rota	21
Duty rosters	22
Roster length	23
Finding your way around the duty rota and roster	23
DRIVING LICENCES	
GENERAL INFORMATION	25
Qualifying for a licence	25
Classes of licence	25
Minimum age limits	26
Cost and duration of licences	27
Renewal and replacement	27
Production of licence	27
PCV DRIVING ENTITLEMENT	27
Categories of PCV entitlement	28
Passenger carrying vehicles	29
PCV driving test	29
Minimum test vehicles	30
Badges	30
Minimum ages of drivers	30
Disciplinary powers of traffic commissioners	31
Production of licence	31
Endorsement and disqualification	31
Transitional arrangements	32
Grandfather rights	33
Preparation for the test	33
Offences	33
CONDITION OF VEHICLES	
CONSTRUCTION AND USE REGULATIONS	34
Definitions	34
Motor vehicle	34
Motor car and heavy motor car	34
Bus	34
Articulated bus	34

Large bus	34
Coach	34
Inter-urban motor coach	34
Long distance touring coach	35
Minibus	35
Trailer	35
Close-coupled	35
Dual-purpose vehicle	35
First used	36
Maximum weights and dimensions	36
Maximum dimensions of buses	36
Manufacturer's plates	37
Twin wheels	37
Speedometers	37
Speed limiters	38
Tachographs	38
Television sets	38
Receiving monitors and videos	38
Performing rights	39
Mirrors	39
Safety glass	39
Windscreen wipers and washers	40
Horns and reversing alarms	40
Fuel tanks	41
Radio interference suppression	41
Smoke	41
Tyres	41
Maintenance of tyres	43
Tyre service and supply	44
Tyre loads and speed ratings	44
Doors	44
Seat belts and anchorage points	44
Rear seat belts	45
Seat belts on coaches	46
Wearing of seat belts	46
Trailers	47
Maximum laden weights	47
Unbraked trailer (markings)	48
Detached trailers	48
Length of tow rope	48
Carriage of passengers in trailers	48
PSVs drawing trailers	48

Brakes	49
Parking brake	49
Main and secondary brakes	49
Retarders	50
Braking efficiencies	50
Application of trailer brakes	51
Turning circles and cut out	51
Cut out (swept circle)	52
Articulated buses	52
Roof strength of coaches	52
Noise	52
LIGHTING	52
Restrictions	52
Use of headlamps and auxiliary lamps	53
Front fog lamps	53
High intensity rear fog lamps	53
Direction indicators	54
Emergency and other services' vehicles	54
Stop lights, reversing lights and trailer lights	55
Use of hazard warning lights	55
Lights required during daylight hours	55
Lights required on stationary vehicles at night	56
General requirements	56
Number plates	56
VEHICLE CERTIFICATION APPROVAL INSPECTION AND ANNUAL TESTING	
Certification of Initial Fitness	57
Vehicle inspections	57
Inspections of PSVs	58
Weighing of buses etc	59
Vehicle testing	60
Summary	60
FITNESS, EQUIPMENT AND USE OF PSVs AND MINIBUSES	
PSV CONDITIONS OF FITNESS	62
Stability	62
Brakes	63
Fuel tanks	64
Silencers and noise	65
Exhaust pipes	65
Electrical equipment	65

Body and suspension	66
Luggage racks	66
Artificial lighting	66
Steps	66
Entrances and exits	67
Doors	68
Access to exits	69
Seating	70
Courier seats	71
Driver's accommodation	71
Ventilation	71
Windscreens	72
Signals	72

EQUIPMENT OF PSVs
Fire extinguishers and first aid	72

USE OF PSVs 73
Obstruction of entrances, exits and gangways	73
Obstruction of driver	73
Body maintenance	73
Lamps	73
Power operated doors	73
Filling of petrol tank	73
Carriage of conductors	73
Carriage of flammable or dangerous substances	73
Markings	74

MINIBUS CONDITIONS OF FITNESS 74
Definition	74
Drivers' responsibility for compliance	74
Doors	75
Seats	76
Electrical connections	76
Fuel tanks and exhaust pipes	76
Step lights	76
General	76

DRIVERS' HOURS AND RECORD KEEPING 77

OFFENCES 78
Prohibition of certain types of payment	78

"COMMUNITY REGULATED" JOURNEYS 78
Daily driving period	79
Weekly driving	79
Driving periods	79

Total fortnightly driving	79
Driving time	80
Breaks from driving	80
Daily rest period	80
Weekly rest period	81
Emergencies	82
Periodic checks	82
Exemptions	82
Summary of EC drivers' hours regulations for PSVs	83
AETR	84
BRITISH DOMESTIC OPERATIONS	85
Operations covered	85
Domestic hours limits	85
Maximum total daily driving time	85
Continuous driving without a break	86
Maximum daily duty/spreadover	86
Daily intervals of rest	86
Minimum weekly rest	87
Driving time	87
Light vans and dual-purpose vehicles	87
Emergencies	87
PSV drivers' hours — domestic	88
MIXED DRIVING	88
What counts as duty?	88
Duty time	89
Two or more employers	90
Exemptions from British domestic hours regulations for part time drivers	90
DRIVERS' HOURS OF WORK RECORDS	90
The tachograph	90
Instrument checks	93
The chart	94
Drivers' responsibilities	95
Two or more employers	97
Employers' responsibilities	97
Records used in evidence	98
Offences	98
Reminders	98
Service timetable and duty roster	99
Exemptions	100
RESPONSIBILITIES OF THE DRIVER	101

CUSTOMER CARE — UNDERSTANDING AND HELPING PASSENGERS 101
Passenger relations 101
The driver's image 101
Understanding passengers 102
Product knowledge 103
Communication 103
When things go wrong 103
Dealing with complaints 104
Summary 104

CONDUCT OF DRIVERS, PASSENGERS, ETC 104
Drivers 104
Conductors and passengers 105
Drivers, inspectors or conductors 105
Smoking 105
Microphones 105
Passengers on PSVs 106
Animals 106
Bulky, dangerous or cumbersome articles 106
Payment of fares 107
Tickets 107
Removal of passengers from the bus 108
The obligation to carry passengers 108
Lost property 109
Standing passengers 109
Seating capacity 110
Alcohol on coaches 110
Designated sports grounds and sporting events 110
England and Wales 110
Scotland 111
Cleanliness of vehicles 112

FARES 113
Revenue protection 113
Inspections 113
Waybills 114
Data 114
Fare tables 114
Tickets 115
Off bus ticket sales 115
Stage numbers 115
Passes and permits 115
Electronic ticket issuing machines 116

vii

Smartcards	116

ACCIDENTS AND INSURANCE

ACCIDENTS	118
Accident forms	119
Company procedures	119
INSURANCE	120
Compulsory cover	120
Production of insurance certificates	121
DRIVING OFFENCES	122
DRINK AND DRIVING	122
Breath tests and laboratory tests	122
DISQUALIFICATION	123
OFFENCES FOR WHICH PENALTY POINTS ARE AWARDED	124
OFFENCES FOR WHICH FINES ARE IMPOSED	126
REMOVAL OF DISQUALIFICATION	130
REMOVAL OF ENDORSEMENTS	131
DUAL LIABILITY	131
USE OF VEHICLES ON THE ROAD	132
SPEED LIMITS	132
Particular speed limits for certain classes of vehicle	132
Exemptions from speed limits	133
Coach speeds driving standards	133
CODE OF CONDUCT	133
Background	133
Scope of code	134
Provisions of code	134
USE OF CAR TELEPHONES AND/OR MICROPHONES	136
DRIVING ON MOTORWAYS	136
Rules	136
Conduct on motorways	137
Motorway signals	137
Driving in fog on motorways	138
Prohibitions	138
Breakdowns	138
Condition of vehicles	139

PEDESTRIAN CROSSINGS AND BUS LANES, ETC	139
Zebra crossings	139
Pelican crossings	140
Bus lanes	140
"Red Routes"	140
De-criminalisation of parking offences in London	140
PARKING RESTRICTIONS	141
Loading and unloading hours	141
No waiting and parking	141
Breakdown and removal of vehicles	142
Parking meters	142
Traffic wardens	142
Fixed penalty system	142
Parking on the road at night without lights	145

Whilst every care has been taken in the preparation of this book, readers should be aware that only Acts of Parliament and Statutory Instruments have the force of law and that they can only be authoritatively interpreted by the courts.

INTRODUCTION

The de-regulation of the bus industry which was completed by the Transport Act 1985 has seen the entry of many new operators. Although London was not included in the deregulation of 1985 it is the Government's intention that bus services in the capital should be de-regulated by 1996.

In many areas high-frequency minibus services have emerged, employing drivers who are new to Public Service Vehicle (PSV) work. Existing PSV drivers are finding themselves allocated to duties such as the operation of a registered local service about which they know little, having previously worked exclusively on school contracts and private hires.

There is, therefore, a great need for a book such as this, which employers can issue to their drivers and which owner-drivers and small operators can carry with them.

Despite the term "de-regulation", the industry is in fact now more regulated than ever! Current legislation demands a great deal of both operator and driver.

To the driver these demands are most exacting and require considerable skill and practical knowledge, especially considering the enormous responsibility of driving passengers.

In addition to driving skills the driver needs a good general knowledge of the various orders and regulations.

The aim of this book is to assist all bus, coach and minibus drivers by putting into plain language an outline of the complex and complicated legislation to which they are subject.

In order to keep the information to reasonable proportions and in "layman's" terms, detailed references to acts, orders and regulations are omitted. If readers wish to improve their knowledge of transport law or the various statutory instruments, the use of the companion book *Croner's Coach & Bus Operations* is recommended. Included in this third edition are details of the new unified Driver Licensing system and the 1990 "Conduct" regulations, etc.

Finally, I hope that this modest introduction to PSV law will encourage some drivers to consider studying the subject in greater depth to improve even further their professional competence.

P FAWCETT

Printed for the Publishers, Croner Publications Ltd,
Croner House, London Road, Kingston upon Thames, Surrey KT2 6SR by
Hobbs the Printers of Southampton.

OPERATORS' LICENCES

Before any operator can use a vehicle with nine or more passenger seats to carry passengers for hire or reward he must have a PSV operator's licence ("O" licence).

Hire or reward includes both carriage at separate fares and carriage of a party at a composite fare (private hire).

Any vehicle with eight or fewer passenger seats which carries passengers at separate fares will also have to be specified on a PSV "O" licence.

"Separate fare" covers all payments made by individual passengers, even if not made directly to the driver or operator. For example, an admission ticket for an event which confers a right to be carried on a vehicle to and from the event will be a separate fare and the operator will require a PSV "O" licence.

Where free transport is provided, for example by a firm's "personnel carrier", no "O" licence is needed. But where a business, such as a hotel, uses a passenger carrying vehicle in association with its main activities (in this illustration, as a "courtesy coach") hire or reward exists. (*Rout v Swallow Hotels 1992*) and the operator must have an "O" licence.

CAR SHARING

The practice of sharing a car or van with eight or fewer seats, for example by employees commuting to the same workplace, is permitted, provided that the fare or fares paid totals less than the running costs of the vehicle, including depreciation. In such cases, the vehicle is not a PSV, nor is the driver's insurance invalidated by virtue of a "private" vehicle being used "commercially".

GROUP HIRE

Where a party hires a coach or bus from an operator for a lump sum and then shares the cost amongst its members by charging separate fares, technically even if the vehicle has eight or fewer seats it will be a PSV and certain journeys may have to be registered as local services.

However, operation of privately organised trips at separate fares is widespread and many coach drivers convey such parties on a regular basis. To regularise the practice, the Public Passenger Vehicles Act 1981 provides that the hire

will not be construed as carriage at separate fares if the following conditions are met:
  (a) neither the driver, owner nor operator of the vehicle made the arrangements for bringing the party together
  (b) the journey has not been previously advertised to the public at large, except by a notice displayed at a place of work, a church or club, or in a journal circulating mainly amongst the relevant employees, worshippers or club members
  (c) all passengers make substantially the same journey and there are no fare differences according to time or distance travelled.

Some passenger carrying vehicles need not be operated under a PSV "O" licence. These include Local Education Authorities' school buses (even when also available to the public at large), Community Buses, and buses and minibuses operated non-commercially by social, welfare, religious and educational organisations under a permit.

PSV "O" licences are issued to the operator and do not identify the vehicles which are used under them. The operator receives licence discs for the number of vehicle in the fleet and these must be displayed on the vehicles.

TYPES OF LICENCE

There are four types of PSV "O" licence issued by Traffic Commissioners:

Standard — national and international	Green discs
Standard national	Blue discs
Restricted	Orange discs
Special restricted	(issued to taxi/bus operators)

In addition Traffic Commissioners can issue Community Bus Permits and permits for "welfare vehicles" (these latter can also be issued by local authorities and other "designated bodies").

A licence will specify the number of vehicles "in possession" and any further number "to be acquired" (the margin). Any vehicle hired in within the margin of the licence must also display a disc (this may be recovered from an out of service vehicle).

Vehicles temporarily hired in for not more than two weeks may display the disc of the operator from whom they are hired. In this case the operator (not the hirer) remains the "user" of the vehicle, responsible for its legal operation. Holders of restricted licences cannot hire large buses with more than 16 seats from standard licence holders.

Standard licences

These permit the operation of any size of PSV. The operator has to satisfy the Traffic Commissioner that he or she:

(a) has sufficient financial resources to run the vehicles safely — the operator can elect either to maintain them in person or to contract out the maintenance but if it is contracted out, the operator remains responsible for the condition of the vehicles on the road

(b) is of "good repute", ie free of previous convictions relating to the use of a PSV during the last five years

(c) is professionally competent, or employs a professionally competent transport manager. The operator or the manager must have a PSV CPC national qualification, and, for a national/international licence, a PSV CPC international qualification.

Traffic Commissioners may suspend, curtail or revoke a PSV O licence for breaches of the regulations concerning drivers' hours and records, mechanical condition of the vehicle or contravention of any conditions attached to the licence.

Restricted licences

An operator may have a restricted licence which covers PSVs with eight or fewer seats, or PSVs with 9-16 seats, exclusive of the driver's seat, which are used non-commercially. Not more than two PSVs per restricted O-licence may be authorised.

"Non-commercially" in this context is different than in the context of car sharing or permit operation and means any operation which is otherwise than in the course of a business of carrying passengers, or a business conducted by a person whose main occupation is not the operation of PSVs with over eight seats. This would include, for example, the use of a minibus by a taxi firm, whose main business is not PSV operation and whose taxis have 8 or less seats, or a hotelier whose business is accommodating guests, not carrying passengers. Taxi operators are major users of restricted licences. Another major user is the Post Office (which is not limited to a maximum of two Post Buses!). The holder of a restricted licence does not have to prove professional competence.

Special restricted licences

These are issued by Traffic Commissioners to holders of taxi (hackney carriage) licences (but not private hire cars), who apply to run a registered local service. There are no requirements as to good repute, financial standing, or professional competence although the holder has to satisfy the local authority's taxi licensing officer that he or she is a fit person to hold a taxi licence and that the vehicle meets prescribed safety standards.

Traffic Commissioners may attach to a special restricted licence a condition that it be used as a PSV only to run a registered local service within the area of the appropriate local licensing authority. When used as a PSV the driver will come within the scope of the domestic drivers' hours regulations but will not need to hold a PCV category D driving entitlement.

Permits

Permits may be issued by Traffic Commissioners to operators of small buses (9–16 seats) and large buses (over 17 seats). Designated bodies (eg the Scouts Association) may issue them to operators of small buses only.

Permit vehicles, which are used mainly by voluntary organisations such as Community Transport and schools and colleges, may be used to carry passengers for hire and reward provided that:

(a) the organisation holding the permit operates the vehicle
(b) it is not available to the public at large
(c) it is being used non-commercially (ie not for profit)
(d) it is being used in accordance with any conditions on the permit

The driver must be over 21 and hold a full current category B driving licence.

A "Permit" disc must be displayed on the vehicle.

Community Bus permits A Community Bus is a vehicle with 9–16 seats operated by a group or groups of persons concerned with the social and welfare needs of a community.

Traffic Commissioners can issue Community Bus permits to allow the operators to provide a local service on a non-commercial basis and to carry passengers in other circumstances (eg private hire) to provide revenue to support the Community Bus service.

The driver must be a volunteer aged 21 years or over and may not receive any payment other than expenses (including loss of earnings). A Community Bus disc must be displayed on the vehicle.

Any local service provided for the public at large by the Community Bus must be registered or, in London, provided under a London local service licence.

NB Drivers aged 18 years or over who hold a full category D driving entitlement may drive a Community Bus or "Permit" minibus with 9-16 seats (but **not** a large "Permit" bus with 17 or more seats until they reach the age of 21).

RUNNING A LOCAL SERVICE

EFFECTS OF DE-REGULATION
Anyone holding a PSV "O" licence may, on giving 42 days' notice to the Traffic Commissioners, register and run a local service outside London. A service may be withdrawn on giving a similar period of notice. Local Education Authorities running school buses, holders of Community Bus permits and holders of taxi licences who have obtained a Special Restricted PSV "O" licence may also register a local service.

No monopoly
Thus the operator of a local service, even if operating this under a service subsidy agreement for which he or she has successfully tendered, is completely unprotected against competition on the route.

Reaction to competition
Drivers who observe other operators on their routes often quite naturally fear for their livelihood, and sometimes respond to competition in illegal ways.

Powers of Traffic Commissioners
This can be counter-productive as Traffic Commissioners have powers to stop an operator running a local service and/or impose a "fine" by reducing the fuel tax rebate if the operator or an employee can be shown to have "intentionally" interfered in the running of another operator's local service.

Drivers' behaviour on the road
It is, therefore, imperative that drivers behave responsibly and do nothing to jeopardise their employer's licence. Competition can only be met legitimately on quality of service, so reliability, timekeeping, good driving and attention to passengers' needs are more important than ever following de-regulation.

Practices such as racing competitors to stops, cutting in or blocking in their vehicles can achieve nothing and must not be resorted to.

LOCAL SERVICES

A local service is any service on which a passenger can travel a distance of less than 15 miles measured in a straight line.

Outside London, as explained above, anyone holding a PSV licence can register a local service.

London local service licences

Within Greater London, a London local service can only be operated either by agreement with London Regional Transport (such agreements usually result from successfully tendering for a service) or under a London local service licence granted by the South Eastern and Metropolitan Traffic Commissioner. These licences are extremely difficult to obtain. Applications are published, objections and representations are heard at public inquiries and the licence is only granted if the Traffic Commissioner considers it in the public interest to do so. The licence gives an operator a monopoly on the route.

Timings

Once an operator has registered a local service it must be run in accordance with the registration. Failure to do so, or operation of an unregistered service, can be sufficient reason for a Traffic Commissioner to consider attaching a condition to the "O" licence preventing the operator from running that, or any other, local service.

It may be tempting to adjust timings in response to competition; for example, in order to run just ahead of a competitor's vehicle. Drivers should bear in mind that although "insignificant" changes of not more than five minutes in the timing of a registered service can be made without notification to the Traffic Commissioner, they cannot be made on a day to day basis, and, once made, must be observed for a reasonable time, so that passengers can adjust to them.

Retiming of school journeys Sometimes an operator is asked by a school to retime a journey (eg to accommodate an early finish or because of industrial action). This may be done if the service is a dedicated school service paid for by the Local Education Authority but only at the request of the LEA and only for the purpose of enabling the LEA to fulfil its duty to provide free school transport. If the timing of any other requested service on which school children rely is altered, the service must still be operated on its registered timing for the benefit of the public at large.

Duplication
Duplication of a service is permitted but only to provide extra journeys over the whole or part of the route so long as they are timed as closely as possible to journeys in the registered timetable.

Traffic regulation conditions
Traffic Commissioners sometimes make traffic regulation conditions to reduce the risks of severe traffic congestion or prevent danger to road users. These conditions may be attached to an operator's licence and drivers should be aware of them and observe them meticulously. A typical condition may be a ban on picking up or setting down in streets in the immediate vicinity of a bus station, in order to persuade operators to use the bus station and not cause congestion on its approaches.

Bus stations and bus stops
Bus stations are usually operated by Passenger Transport Executives (PTEs) or local authorities, although some remain in private hands. Bus station operators can make departure changes and allocate stands, although they are legally required to do so as fairly as possible and not to favour any particular operator. Drivers should co-operate with PTE and local authority inspectors when using bus stations. In particular they should be prepared to move their vehicle from a stand if asked to do so and should avoid interfering with the manoeuvring of competitors' vehicles in the bus station. If their freedom of movement is compromised they should inform both the bus station inspector and their employer.

Bus stops are the responsibility of the local highway authority (County Councils, or, in Scotland, Regional Councils) and, in Metropolitan Areas, the PTE. Highway authorities may also make local traffic regulation orders, for example to control picking up and setting down points for excursions and tours, or to limit layover time in city centre kerbside stops.

Hail and ride

The advent of high-frequency urban minibus services has been accompanied by the introduction of services which do not observe bus stops but pick up on being hailed and set down on request. Drivers on such services must only observe hail and ride working on those sections of the route which the Traffic Commissioner has agreed to register for that purpose. When driving a hail and ride service it is more important than ever to show courtesy to other road users and avoid sudden and unsignalled stops, or stopping at dangerous points such as on the brow of a hill, in proximity to a road junction or on a bend.

Faretables, timetables and destination notices

Operators must display on a vehicle used on a registered service, or make available on such a vehicle:

(a) the fare table
(b) the timetable.

Destination indicators must be displayed clearly on the exterior of a vehicle used on a registered service.

These conditions do not apply to taxis used on a special restricted "O" licence or to excursions and tours.

Taxis

A taxi (but not a licensed private hire car) may register and run a local service if the operator has obtained a special restricted operator's licence.

In addition taxis may be hired at separate fares from authorised places, ie specially designated ranks, at which taxis to common destinations may ply for hire. They must display a "Shared Taxi" sign, and *may not* ply for hire at separate fares by cruising along a bus route but the driver may "tout" for business at the designated ranks. He must do so in an orderly way, by word of mouth only, and within 6m of his taxi.

Taxis and private hire cars may also be pre-booked at separate fares.

Drivers of PSVs should not interfere with taxi operators but may report any transgressors of the above rules to the local taxi licensing officer, or, in the case of the operator of a taxi or bus running a local service, to the Traffic Commissioner.

Fuel tax rebates

Operators of local services receive rebates of fuel tax. If the Traffic Commissioner finds that they have intentionally interferred in the operation of another operator's local service, or failed to operate a local service as requested, or run an unregistered local service, then the Commissioner has powers under the Transport Act 1985 to make one or both of the following orders:

(a) *section 26 order*, prohibiting the operation of a specified or any local service
(b) *section 111 order*, determining that the operator repay 20% of his fuel tax rebate over the previous three months.

COMPETITION LAW

Since bus de-regulation, competition law now applies to the bus industry in exactly the same way as it applies to traders in the High Street.

Any agreement made between two or more operators in which they voluntarily accept restrictions on their ability to compete is registerable with, and comes under the scrutiny of, the Office of Fair Trading (OFT). This will include any agreements on joint operations, tendering, ticketing or route sharing. The OFT may of course decide that the agreement is not potentially harmful to the public or designed to exclude a competitor and permit it.

Unfair competitive practices, especially the practice known as "predatory pricing" where a large operator drops bus fares to an uneconomic level to drive a competitor off "his" route can also be investigated by the OFT.

Drivers should be on the look out for restrictive and anti-competitive practices and report these to their employers, or complain to the OFT.

TENDERED SERVICES

In the past, schools contracts have been many an operator's bread and butter. Now these, together with any socially desirable services which no operator has registered because takings are too low, are put out to tender by County and Regional (in Scotland) Councils and PTEs (in Metropolitan Areas).

Drivers operating tendered services should be especially vigilant to ensure that no journeys are lost and must report any lost mileage immediately. Failure to do so can result in loss of the service subsidy contract.

In addition, some tenders are won on the basis of quoting for a service operating cost with the tendering authority retaining the revenue. In such instances drivers must be able to account fully for all revenue, especially if their vehicle is boarded by a tendering authority's inspector.

CONCESSIONARY FARES

County, District and Regional Councils and, in Metropolitan Areas, PTEs, have powers to make concessionary fares schemes for: pensioners; children under 17; scholars age 17-19; blind and disabled persons. These may take the form of free travel, tokens, or permits allowing reduced fares either all day or at off peak times.

The above authorities also have powers to serve compulsory participation notices to operators providing local services in their area.

Drivers should familiarise themselves with their local concessionary fares schemes and co-operate in implementing them. In particular they must permit inspectors and data collectors employed by the above authorities to board their buses to make fare checks and collect data.

COMMUNITY TRANSPORT

Vehicles operated by Community Transport organisations do carry passengers at separate fares. However, drivers should be aware that services such as Disabled Dial a Ride are not in competition since:

(a) they are not available to the public at large
(b) they are operated under the minibus permit regulations and
(c) they are frequently subsidised by the local authority or PTE.

SCHEDULES AND DUTIES

The provision of a public passenger transport service is not a "nine to five" job.

In the case of some local urban and inter-urban services the first vehicle often leaves the depot before dawn and the last vehicle arrives back at the depot close to midnight. In express service operation, nights out for both vehicles and crews are not uncommon. Inevitably, unsociable hours have to be worked.

Scheduling a fleet of vehicles and allocating staff to them so as to provide the best service in the most economical manner is an art. The scheduler produces an interdependent set of timetables, individual vehicle timings, a duty roster and a rota of individuals' daily duties.

Drivers do not need to be able to prepare these documents but it is essential that they can read and understand them. The smooth working of the undertaking relies on staff reporting for duty punctually, relieving earlier drivers or crews at the right time and following the instructions on the vehicle running board.

Schedules not only affect drivers' working lives but their social and domestic lives as well. Workable schedules and rotas which staff perceive to be "fair" improve drivers' working conditions and help retain a satisfied and well motivated staff. This in turn leads to a better and more reliable service to the public and enhances employees' job security. This is especially important in the competitive post deregulation world.

The service timetable

Many operators issue their drivers with copies of the service timetables which they also make available to the public. In any case one of the conditions attached to registration of a local service is that the timetable and faretable are carried or displayed on the vehicle.

Often the vehicle running board will only show timings at route termini and perhaps one or two main points en route and the service timetable is then the only means the driver has of knowing his expected time at intermediate points.

Delays to service are often inescapable but running ahead of time is inexcusable. Apart from possible disciplinary action against the driver, early running can result in loss of revenue through missed passengers, loss of passenger goodwill, or the danger that the undertaking may be reported to the Traffic Commissioners for failing to provide a service as registered, which could lead to sanctions against the operator's licence.

Drivers who are detailed to run a duplicate service should also be aware of, and try to comply with, the rules which Traffic Commissioners are applying to such services. These are that duplication should only take place to provide extra journeys over the whole or part of the route and that these journeys should be timed to run as closely as possible to the registered timetable.

Failure to comply with these simple rules could, wherever there is a competing service on the route, be construed as interference in the operation of another registered service.

The service timetable may employ either the 24 hour clock or am/pm timings.

Conventionally the timing points on the route are listed down a column at the left hand side of the page and the timings for each journey are given in further columns to the right of this. Separate tables are prepared for journeys in either direction and sometimes for Saturdays, Sundays and Bank Holidays, or summer and winter services.

Example of Greater Manchester Buses Ltd Standard Timetable

STALYBRIDGE – OLDHAM

Mondays to Saturdays

	NS	NS				NS					
STALYBRIDGE, Bus Station	0715	0745	0845		1645	1715	1745	1845	1945		2245
Stamford Park	0718	0748	0848	AND	1648	1718	1748	1848	1948	AND	2248
Hurst Cross	0722	0752	0852	EVERY	1652	1722	1752	1852	1952	EVERY	2252
Abbeyhills, Welcome Inn	0730	0800	0900	HOUR	1700	1730	1800	1900	1958	HOUR	2258
OLDHAM, Town Square	0738	0808	0908	UNTIL	1708	1738	1808	1908	2006	UNTIL	2306

Sundays

STALYBRIDGE, Bus Station	1345		2245
Stamford Park	1348	AND	2248
Hurst Cross	1352	EVERY	2252
Abbeyhills, Welcome Inn	1358	HOUR	2258
OLDHAM, Town Square	1406	UNTIL	2306

NS – Not Saturdays

Codes at the head of each column give additional information. Standard abbreviations are M, T, W, Th, F, S, Su for the days of the week, plus the letters X for excepted and O for only, thus:

MO = Mondays only
SSuX = Saturdays and Sundays excepted.

Other letters and symbols are used to indicate journeys which operate:

Schooldays only
Market days only
Bank Holidays only or excepted Summer Sundays, etc.

Codes beside timings may indicate picking up and setting down restrictions, and timing information such as:

u — stops to pick up only
s — stops to set down only
a — arrival time
d — departure time

A few undertakings issue non-conventional timetables with, for example, timings and timing points shown in rows rather than columns (see below), or with lists of departure times from main points with running times in minutes to intermediate points. Whilst these are brief and less bulky than conventional timetables they are also more difficult to use for both drivers and passengers.

Example of Time Table in Columnar Form

BUS STN	RAIL STN	NEAR TOWN	FAR TOWN
0900	0905	0915	0928
1000	1005	1015	1028
1100	1105	1115	1128
1200	1205	1215	1228
1300	1305	1315	1328

The bus running board

Whilst the service timetable shows all the journeys made by all the vehicles on the route, the running boards which are prepared for each vehicle show only the specific journeys made by that vehicle.

Since some service buses may be on the road for as long as 18 hours and may make journeys on more than one service, the same running board may be used in the course of a day by more than one driver. As it relates primarily to the work done by the bus and only incidentally to some or all of the driver's duties it should be left on the vehicle.

Running boards often contain a mass of information not shown on the service timetable, for example descriptions of turning manoeuvres to be performed at termini, instructions to run "dead" or out of service between certain trips, or between depot and termini, or details of timed connections to be made (eg at a rail station).

Example of Running Board
(Greater Manchester Buses Ltd)

Days of Operation	Leave Depot		Running Board No.
WEEKDAYS	0630		1

Service No.	1	1	2	2	1	1	2	2	1	1	2	2	1	1	2	2	1	1
BUS STATION	0625	0615	0630	0830	0835	0915	0930	1030	1035	1115	1130	1130	1235	1315	1330	1430	1435	1515
MOOR HILL	0658	0703	↓	↑	0858	0903	↓	↑	1058	1103	↓	↑	1258	1303	↓	↑	1458	1503
MILL GATE			0743	0818			0943	1018			1143	1218			1243	1418		
LITTLEFOLD			0758	0803			0958	1003			1158	1203			1258	1403		

Service No.	2	2	1	1	2	2	1	1	2	2	1	1	2	2	1	1		
BUS STATION	1530	1630	1635	1715	1730	1830	1835	1915	1930	2030	2035	2115	2130	2230	2235	2315	2330	
MOOR HILL	↓	↑	1658	1703	↓	↑	1858	1903	↓	↑	2058	2103	↓	↑	2258	2303		
MILL GATE	1543	1618			1743	1818			1943	2018			2143	2218				
LITTLEFOLD	1558	1603			1758	1803			1958	2003			2158	2203				
																	↓	
DEPOT																	2335	

From	To	Duty	
0630	1025	4	
1025	1330	3	
1330	1825	33	
1825	2335	11	

There are many different running board formats. Nowadays these are often computer print-outs. Usually, like the service timetable, they have timing points in the left hand column, and timings of each trip in columns to the right of this. There the similarities end. Timings in both directions are usually shown, reading both up and down columns. Arrows are frequently used to indicate the direction of travel of the vehicle.

Some running boards have timing points at the head of each column and times in rows below these. A few operators produce running boards which could more accurately be described as "duty boards" since they contain details of all the trips to be performed by a driver on a specific duty. These can be removed from one vehicle and taken to the next vehicle to be driven (perhaps after a meal break) since they are essentially a consolidation of extracts from the running boards of all the vehicles to be driven in that duty.

Example of a Duty Board (*Ribble Motor Services*)

```
| WARWICK SYSTEMS   | EMPLOYEE NO   | REPTD.  | REF.   MILES   | DUTY NO : KE 3    |
|                   |               |         | 554    27.3    |                   |
| OFF  1549         | DRIVERS NAME  | INTLS.  | 555    86.5    | DAYS : MON TO FRI |
| ON   0652         |               |         |                | KENDAL            |
| TIME 8.57 OT 1.09 | DATE :        | REPTD.  |                | VALID FROM :      |
|                   | DAY  :        |         |                | 01/12/86          |
|                   |               | INTLS.  |                |                   |
|                   | ROTA :        |         | TOTAL : 113.8  |                   |
```

```
    MILES   REF     SERV  ARR            POINT                    DEP        NOTES
                            BUS DUTY 2    KE                                 BUS NO. ......
            555     555          KENDAL BUS STATION              0657
                           0725 WINDERMERE                       0727
                           0742 AMBLESIDE RIBBLE BUS STN         0745
    31.3    555     555    0837 KESWICK BUS STATION              0845
                           0933 AMBLESIDE RIBBLE BUS STN         0940
                           0955 WINDERMERE                       0959
    30.6                   1024 KENDAL BUS STATION
                           RELIEF FOR 1026 SERVICE 555   TO LANCASTER BUS STATION

                            BUS DUTY 3    KE                                 BUS NO. ......
            555     556          KENDAL BUS STATION              1256
                           1320 MILNTHORPE SQUARE                1320        SEE NOTE 1
    24.6    554     554    1410 LANCASTER BUS STATION            1415
                           1524 MILNTHORPE SQUARE                1524
    27.3                   1549 KENDAL BUS STATION
                           RELIEF FOR 1550 SERVICE 554   TO CARNFORTH NEW STREET

    1 VIA PRIEST HUTTON
```

There are a number of points which drivers can bear in mind when studying their running boards.
1. **Interworking** — a vehicle may be switched from one route to another in order to maximise its productivity. For

example, a works journey to an industrial estate may be linked with a following school journey from an adjacent housing estate.

A more usual reason for switching vehicles between routes is to reduce the total number of vehicles required. Where two routes meet at a common point, such as a bus station, and the total of all the "layovers" or slack times of all the vehicles on the two routes would be sufficient to perform a complete round trip, the vehicles may be rescheduled to interwork the two routes and save a vehicle. It is important of course that a minimum agreed layover time still remains for each vehicle at its trip end.

2. **Tidal flow operation** — at peak times when the majority of passengers are travelling in one direction, eg into town in the morning peak, it makes sense to maximise the number of vehicles in service in that direction. Some vehicles can be scheduled to run back to outer termini "out of service" so as to be available there more quickly and perform an additional inward journey which will still be in the peak hour. For the sake of good passenger relations it is essential that the vehicle destination blinds on light trips clearly indicate that the vehicle is not in service.

3. **Drop back vehicles** — a vehicle may be brought out of depot to perform one round trip on a service and this journey may be included in part of a driver's duty. Although this is often done simply to duplicate journeys at times of peak demand, two other reasons for slotting a "drop back" into a service are:

   (a) to enable a service affected by congestion to recover. The extra bus is slotted into the service at the start of the morning or evening peak and all buses on the route "drop back" to the timing of the following vehicle. By the time the extra bus has performed a round trip it will arrive back at the point where it was slotted in simultaneously with a service bus and can be run back to depot

   (b) to cover meal breaks. The extra bus takes over the journey which the driver taking the meal break would have done. All buses on the service then drop back as described above, enabling their drivers to take a meal break equivalent to the headway between vehicles. The drop back bus or buses can be returned to depot when all meal breaks have been completed.

For example — if the round trip running time (including five minutes layover at each end of the route) on a service run with four vehicles is 60 minutes, departures from the bus station could be at:

> Bus No. 1   00 minutes past the hour
> Bus No. 2   15 minutes past the hour
> Bus No. 3   30 minutes past the hour
> Bus No. 4   45 minutes past the hour
> Bus No. 1   00 minutes past the next hour

Inserting an extra bus on the hour allows bus No. 1 to take over the 15 minutes past departure, No. 2 the 30 minutes past etc. On the next hour, Bus No. 4 and the extra bus will arrive simultaneously at the bus station, and the extra bus can be returned to depot without destroying the basic 15 minute headway on the service.

4. **Frequency changes** — lower frequencies are usually provided between peak periods, in the evenings and on Sundays. At the times when frequencies are changed the driver may notice that the pattern of departure times from termini alters. For example, with departures on the hour and every 20 minutes a change from three to two buses per hour will change the departures at 20 and 40 minutes past the hour to one at half past the hour.
5. **Differential running times** — whilst it is often difficult to run to time in the peak hours, it is also often frustrating for both drivers and passengers if time has to be spent in the off peak at timing points to avoid running early. For this reason the running times allowed on a route are sometimes adjusted at different times of the day to take account of traffic congestion and heavier passenger loadings.

CREW ALLOCATION

The United Kingdom and EC drivers' hours regulations set an upper limit on the amount of work which can be allocated daily and weekly to drivers.

Daily limits
The maximum length of time for which a driver on domestic journeys and work (which includes all regular local services)

can drive without taking a break of at least 30 minutes is 5½ hours. This may be extended to 8½ hours if the total of all the breaks in that period is not less than 45 minutes. The maximum total driving time is 10 hours. The working day must not exceed 16 hours and the driver must normally have 10 hours' rest between working days; this may be reduced to 8½ hours on three occasions each week.

On Community regulated duties (mainly express and private hire work) the maximum aggregate driving time without a break of at least 45 minutes is 4½ hours. The maximum total daily driving time is normally nine hours but can be 10 hours twice in a fixed week. The driver must have 11 hours' rest in every 24 hours; this may be reduced to nine hours on three occasions per week if the lost rest is compensated for by the end of the following week. The minimum daily rest if the vehicle is double manned is eight hours in every 30 hours.

Weekly limits

Domestic drivers must have a fortnightly rest of 24 hours, and Community regulated drivers must have a weekly rest of 45 hours after six consecutive days' driving, although there are complicated relaxations of this rule.

The above is a necessarily brief resumé of the drivers' hours limits which affect the allocation of drivers and crews to vehicles. Full details are given under *Drivers' Hours*.

In addition to statutory limits on hours of work, many drivers are covered by trade union agreements which also affect their duties. These generally cover matters outside the statutory limits, such as the maximum number of "split" duties to be included within a roster and travelling times between relief points and the place where meal breaks are taken.

Driving duties

Duties are usually arranged in such a way that a driver is allocated to a vehicle in service for a portion of its time on the road before being relieved for a meal break. After his meal break the driver is then allocated to another vehicle for the remainder of his duty.

Overtime

In making up duties, schedulers sometimes leave small portions of work unallocated, to be staffed on an overtime basis.

Allocators and drivers have a duty to ensure that in detailing a driver to, or volunteering for, such an overtime portion, none of the following are exceeded or encroached upon:
- maximum daily driving time
- daily spreadover limits
- minimum daily rest periods
- minimum weekly or fortnightly rest periods
- limits on "mixed" domestic or community driving where these apply (see *Drivers' Hours*).

Some undertakings have negotiated standard weekly payments for drivers which equate with an average week's work on a roster containing some scheduled overtime. The rosters are arranged to even out the work done over a fixed period. Rest day working (see below) is usually still voluntary and not included in this averaging.

Types of duty

To cover all the services in a full working day some staff will have to start work early and could be coming off duty even before midday, others will have to start late and work through to nearly midnight and yet others will be needed to cover the work in the middle of the day. In addition, because there will be extra vehicles out in the morning and evening peaks, some staff will need to perform split duties, with a period off duty between their two periods of work. A roster (see below) is drawn up and posted well in advance to spread this work on a rota basis and to acquaint staff with their personal duty patterns for the coming months.

Trade union agreements usually define different types of duties in some way so that allocators and staff know the time boundaries within which they are working. A typical agreement would be:

Early duty: Finishing no later than 15.30
Middle duty: Finishing no later than 20.00
Late duty: Finishing after 20.00
Split duty: Covering two work portions (usually in the morning and evening peak periods) and with an intermediate off duty period. This may be "paid through" and be of some duration between maximum and minimum limits, eg over $1\frac{1}{2}$ but less than four hours.

THE DEPOT'S DAILY DUTY ROTA

Size of the rota

An estimate of the number of duties which will have to be worked by the staff at a depot in order to drive all the vehicles in service can be made by dividing the total number of bus hours by the average work content (ie ignoring signing on and off times, meal breaks and any time spent by a driver travelling on foot or as a passenger to take over a bus).

Linking portions of work together in the most economic way so as to get the most productivity from bus drivers or crews is an art; the result being the list of numbered duties which are posted in the depot; usually in strict order of their starting times.

A typical duty line on a rota may look like this:

Extract from Duty Rota

Duty No.	Sign on	Take over		Bus No.	Relieved		Sign Off	Hours	Pay
		Time	Place		Time	Place			
M.1	1210	1230	Bus Stn	3	1615	Bus Stn			
		1645	Bus Stn	2	1940	Bus Stn			
		1945	Stand 1	4	1950	Garage	2000	7.50	8.00

Notes: M.1 — this is classed as a middle duty.

Sign on 12.10 — as well as a signing on time allowance to enable the driver to collect a ticket machine, make up a waybill, etc to find, check and take over the bus allocated to running board 3 and if necessary set the destination blinds, there may be an additional travelling allowance to enable the driver to reach the take-over point if this is, as in this case, not the depot where he or she signs on.

16.15 to 16.45 — meal break and statutory break. Take over Bus 2 at 16.45 in the bus station.

19.40 to 19.45 — take over Bus 4. The five minutes allowed may include a couple of minutes travelling time to an adjacent stand, perhaps in the street outside the bus station.

19.50 — both the bus and the driver return to depot. 10 minutes signing off allowance given.

7.50 — time from signing on to signing off.

8.00 — time value of the duty for payment purposes. In

this case it probably represents a negotiated minimum day's pay.

Note that the meal break is also "paid through" in this case. In some organisations, "paid through" spreadover duties have been negotiated. In others, payment may be at time and a half because of factors like Sunday working, extra late finishing, etc.

Standby duties are also written into the rota so that the signing on and off times are known. Usually these correspond roughly to the type of duty which the relief replaces in the roster pattern. Occasionally there are portions of duties which contain no work content (eg the second half of a late duty) and these may be marked on the rota with an instruction such as "Enquire" which indicates that the driver can be asked to stand by for that time period.

Sometimes if the depot is fully staffed and there are no obvious problems the allocator or inspector may allow the driver to sign off without incurring any pay penalties.

It may even be in the interests of an allocator to sign a driver off early in order to bring him in early the next day without infringing his statutory daily rest allowance.

Drivers should note in this case that although they may be rostered and paid for working until late, so far as their statutory hours are concerned, what counts is the time they are actually on duty, not the time they are rostered.

Duty rosters

In the duty roster which accompanies the rota staff are allocated a numbered duty for every day on which they are scheduled to work. Some rosters are for seven days with an allocated rest day (and the opportunity to work overtime on one rest day per fortnight on domestic work). Others are for five days with certain rest days "starred" to indicate an overtime opportunity. (These are more common where the bulk of weekend work is performed by part time staff.)

To comply with drivers' hours regulations and union agreements rosters are usually drawn up so that a long weekend is scheduled each month and no late duty is followed by an early duty. Some duties are "stand by" duties to cover for sickness and absenteeism, others are "regular reliefs" to cover specific types of duty left uncovered by a driver or crew being scheduled for a rest day.

Roster length The total number of daily duties in a week (ie five times the number of duties on the daily rota plus the Saturday and Sunday rota) divided by the length of the working week gives an indication of the size of the roster. For example, if there are 61 duties in a week and staff work five days, this will give a roster length of 13 weeks with four "spare" or standby duties.

The length of a roster can be reduced by splitting it — for example by allocating a group of drivers to a restricted number of routes. The number of split duties will also depend upon the severity of the peak hour demands in relation to the off peak traffic, in particular the extent to which operating frequencies have to be increased in the peak, or additional traffic can be generated in the off peak to avoid operating too many part time vehicles.

Duty Postings

Name	Week Numbers for weeks commencing:				
	May 4	May 11	May 18	May 25	etc
Smith	1	2	3	4	5
Jones	2	3	4	5	6
Williams	3	4	5	6	7
Green	4	5	6	7	8
etc...					

Finding your way around the duty rota and roster

Drivers normally work their way through the roster to which they are allocated. Thus if in the current week a driver is on week 1 of the roster given as an example below, he or she will work late duties M-F and have S and Su off. The following week he or she will work week 2, having M and Tu off (providing the monthly long weekend) and then commence early duties. Note that for the purposes of drivers' hours this prevents an early duty following a late duty the previous night.

The rota will contain details of the work content of all the duties, so that a driver allocated to M.1 on M and Tu of Week 4 will be able to ascertain that on those days he or she will sign on at 12.10 and sign off at 20.00.

A typical short (12 week) duty roster may look like the example given below. It should be emphasised that this is only an example and is not a model of all rosters. Each individual undertaking will have its own negotiated roster pattern which will contain only some of the features of this example.

Duty schedules and rosters are complicated. They are also sometimes changed at short notice to accommodate traffic irregularities.

Note: if in any doubt as to the duties to be worked on the current or following days it is safer to ask than to risk missing a duty. Not only is this a disciplinary matter, it also affects the reliability of services and could in the long term affect the operator's reputation, operator's licence and even commercial survival and the driver's own job security.

Duty Roster

Week no	M	T	W	Th	F	S	Su
1	L1	L1	L1	L1	L1	*	*
2	*	*	E1	E1	E1	E1	E1
3	E1	E1	*	R	S1	S1	*
4	M1	M1	R	*	*	L1	L1
5	L2	L2	L2	L2	L2	*	*
6	*	*	E2	E2	E2	E2	E2
7	E2	E2	*	S1	R	M1	*
8	S1	R	M1	*	*	L2	L2
9	L3	L3	L3	L3	L3	*	*
10	*	*	E3	E3	E3	E3	M1
11	E3	E3	*	M1	M1	R	*
12	R	S1	S1	*	*	L3	R

Key

* = day off
L = late duties (3 on M-S and 2 on Su)
M = middle duties (1 each day)
E = early duties (3 on M-S and 2 on Su)
S = split duties (1 on M-S)
R = standby or regular relief (1 on each day)
    eg: the relief on week 12 could work the early on week 11 if necessary.

DRIVING LICENCES

GENERAL INFORMATION

Qualifying for a licence
A driving licence may be obtained if, during the past two years the applicant has:
   (a) held a full licence
   (b) passed a driving test
   (c) held a full licence issued in Northern Ireland, the Isle of Man or the Channel Islands.

Classes of licence
1. Provisional licence.
2. Ordinary driving licence.
3. Passenger Carrying Vehicle driving entitlement, replacing Public Service Vehicle licence.
4. Large Goods Vehicle driving entitlement, replacing Heavy Goods Vehicle licence.
5. Visitor's driving licence.
6. International driving permit.

A provisional licence must be obtained in order to take a vehicle on the road for the purpose of learning to drive and taking the regulation test.

The holder of a provisional licence may drive a vehicle only when accompanied by, and under the supervision of, a qualified driver who must be at least 21 years of age and have held a licence for at least 3 years.

Application forms for a provisional licence are obtainable from post offices and when completed should be sent to the Driver and Vehicle Licensing Centre (DVLC) Swansea together with the appropriate fee (see page 27). **Note:** this does not apply to the application for a provisional PCV (category D) licence which is dealt with as a separate item in this section.

There are different categories of vehicles for driving licence purposes (classified A-P) each entitling a driver to drive the vehicles in that class.

A test passed on a vehicle with automatic transmission restricts driving to that type of vehicle. A further test must be taken before driving a vehicle with manual transmission.

A test passed on a moped does not entitle the candidate to a full motorcycle licence.

A test passed on a moped or motorcycle does not entitle the candidate to drive a motor car or heavy vehicle.

It is an offence to drive a vehicle on public road unless the driver holds the appropriate licence for that particular class of vehicle.

The cost of an ordinary driving test is currently £23.50.

Minimum age limits No person under the age of 16 is allowed to drive a motor vehicle on the roads. The minimum ages for driving the various groups of vehicles are:

Moped, engine capacity not exceeding 50cc	16 years
Motor scooter, motorcycle and three-wheel car	17 years
Small passenger vehicle, ie constructed or adapted to carry not more than nine persons including the driver, or *small goods vehicle*, ie constructed or adapted to carry or to haul goods and not adapted to carry more than nine persons including the driver and not exceeding 3.5t permissible maximum weight (including the weight of any trailer drawn not exceeding 750kg gross)	17 years or 16 years if a disabled person receiving a mobility allowance under s.37A of the Social Security Act 1975
Large passenger vehicle, ie constructed or adapted to carry not more than 17 persons including the driver (restricted to within Great Britain); PSVs on regular services of less than 50km in length; "out of service" PSVs; driving a PSV when supervised by a PSV licence holder	18 years
Other motor vehicles, ie public service vehicles, goods vehicles exceeding 7.5 tonnes permissible maximum weight (including the weight of any trailer drawn), articulated vehicles	21 years

The age limits shown do not apply to vehicles owned or driven under orders of HM Forces.

Cost and duration of licences

Full ordinary driving licence granted in exchange for an existing licence £21

Provisional licence (valid until the holder's 70th birthday) with conversion to full licence after passing driving test £21

Exchange licence when additional group of vehicles added £6

Full Passenger Carrying Vehicle (PCV) entitlement £21

Renewal and replacement

A driving licence must be renewed on or before the date of expiry. No days of grace are allowed. Ordinary licences lost or defaced may be replaced at a cost of £6.

Production of licence

A police officer can demand the production of a driving licence for examination and if it is not immediately available it is a defence to show that the driver:
 (a) produced it at a police station of his or her choice within seven days, or
 (b) produced it there as soon as possible, or
 (c) due to circumstances it was not reasonably practicable to produce the licence before the day on which proceedings for not producing the licence were commenced.

(See also page 31 regarding the production of a PSV driver's licence.)

Remember that a driver must have a current ordinary licence with PCV entitlement (where applicable), and this must be signed. This is a legal requirement.

PCV DRIVING ENTITLEMENT

On 1.4.91 the United Kingdom fully implemented the provisions in the Road Traffic (Driver Licences and Information Systems) Act 1989 and the Motor Vehicles (Driving Licences) (Large Goods Vehicles and Passenger Carrying Vehicles) Regulations 1990 SI 2612 which provided for a unified driver licensing system conforming to the requirements of EC Directive 80/1263.

The regulations which bring the United Kingdom into line with European Community practice provide that:

(a) the previous separation of driving licences into vocational licences (issued by Traffic Commissioners from Traffic Area Offices) and ordinary driving licences issued by the DVLC at Swansea ceased subject to there being transitional arrangements covering the currency of existing vocational licences

(b) there is now a unified licence showing driving entitlement for all vehicles issued centrally by DVLC, henceforth the licensing authority for the issue of all driving licences. However, Traffic Commissioners retain their disciplinary powers in relation to drivers of Passenger Carrying Vehicles

(c) higher medical standards are required for PCV drivers — epileptics, diabetics receiving insulin treatment and drivers falling below new eyesight standards (including monocular drivers) will not be issued with PCV licences. (There are some relaxations other than for certain epileptics* who may not receive PCV entitlement in these standards for existing PSV licence holders)

(d) medical reports are required on applying for a PCV entitlement or renewing a PCV entitlement from age 45 onwards. PCV entitlement is valid until age 45; thereafter renewals must be made every five years and annually from the age of 65. There is an obligation for licence holders to notify DVLC if an illness or disability is expected to last more than three months, or worsens, if this is likely to affect their driving.

Categories of PCV entitlement

Category D + E — articulated buses and buses towing trailers.

Category D — large passenger carrying vehicle with nine or more seats.

This category is further subdivided into:

D (9–16 seats) small PCV and

D (5.5m or less) short PCV.

Category D1 — PCVs (minibuses 9–16 seats) not used for hire and reward.

---

* *epileptics may apply for PCV entitlement subject to being able to satisfy certain conditions.*

Passenger carrying vehicles

The regulations no longer refer to PSVs. All buses, whether or not used for hire and reward, are classed as PCVs. Thus a category D or D1 entitlement is required to drive a PCV not used for hire and reward, but a PSV with eight or less seats can now be driven on a Category B entitlement (which covers motor vehicles with eight or less passenger seats not exceeding 3.5t gvw). Drivers of school buses owned by Local Education Authorities (LEAs) require category D entitlement, but not drivers of Community or "Permit" minibuses.

PCV driving test

Drivers must hold a full ordinary car entitlement (Category B) before applying for a licence showing *provisional* Category D (PCV) entitlement. This requirement, called staging, effectively prevents the conduct of dual ordinary/vocational driving tests.

The application must be made to DVLC on Form D2 and can be made up to three months in advance of the licence being required, accompanied by a medical report (Form DTp 20003) which must be signed by a doctor not more than four months prior to the date the licence is to take effect (reg 4 of SI 1991 No 2612) and the fee of £21.

Applications for a PCV driving test are made to DVLC, and should be accompanied by the test fee of £55.50. The test may be conducted by:

(a) a PCV examiner of the Driving Standards Agency appointed by the DOT
(b) an examiner approved by the DOT and delegated by a PSV operator who employs over 250 drivers and has obtained permission to appoint an employee
(c) persons authorised by the armed forces, a fire brigade or police authority for employees engaged in driving their vehicles.

The examiner will test the applicant's competence and in particular will have regard to the following items:
- knowledge of the highway code
- knowledge of components relating to safety of the vehicle
- competence to drive the vehicle and in particular that the driver can:
  - start the engine
  - move off straight ahead and at an angle

- adopt and keep a safe position in respect of the vehicle in front
- overtake safely
- turn right and left
- make an emergency stop, safely
- stop under normal conditions
- reverse into a restricted opening to the right or to the left and stop the vehicle in a predetermined position
- give appropriate signals
- respond and react to traffic signs and signals.

The PCV driving test is now similar in most respects to the LGV driving test in that both are of the same duration (1½ hours) and conducted partly on the public road and partly off it (to test manoeuvring skills).

A driver driving a PCV as a provisional category D licence holder must:

(a) be under the supervision of a full licence holder for that category of PCV
(b) display L plates to the front and rear of the vehicle.

On passing the test a driver will have a full PCV driving entitlement once DVLC receives:

(a) the test pass certificate
(b) the provisional category D licence (for addition of full entitlement).

Minimum test vehicles

A driver with provisional category D entitlement who passes a PCV driving test in a vehicle smaller than a minimum test vehicle will obtain a *category D (9–16 seats)* small PCV licence which will only entitle him to drive a minibus for hire and reward.

A minimum test vehicle must be 8.5m or more in length. From 1.4.94 minimum test vehicles must be 9m or more in length and capable of attaining a speed of 80kph.

The same minimum test vehicle may be used for a category D + E test providing it is drawing a trailer of at least 1250kg.

Badges

There is no longer any requirement for drivers to wear badges.

Minimum ages of drivers

The normal minimum age of drivers of buses is 21, but drivers aged 18 or more may drive a category D vehicle as a properly supervised trainee, whilst taking a test, or whilst the vehicle is not carrying any passengers if they have category D entitlement.

They may drive a PCV used under a PSV Operator's Licence, with passengers, provided the bus is on a regular service where the route is 50km or less or the vehicle is constructed to carry not more than 16 passengers and the journey is within the United Kingdom.

Disciplinary powers of Traffic Commissioners

Traffic Commissioners retain the same disciplinary powers over PCV drivers as they have exercised in the past over PSV drivers. Schedule 2 of the Road Traffic (Driver Licensing and Information Systems) Act 1989 allows for the referral by the Secretary of State for Transport of questions relating to the conduct of applicants for, or holders of, PSV licences or PCV entitlement to the Traffic Commissioner, and where the Commissioner notifies the Secretary of State that the applicant or holder is not in his opinion a fit person to hold a licence, the Secretary of State must refuse to grant, revoke or suspend the licence or disqualify the holder indefinitely or for a determined period.

Appeals against the refusal of the Secretary of State to reconsider refusing an applicant a licence, revoking or suspending a PCV licence or disqualifying a PCV driver can still be made to a magistrate's court (sheriff's court in Scotland), and any Traffic Commissioner to whom the matter was referred then becomes the respondent in the case. PCV drivers must declare all convictions to their local Area Traffic Office.

A traffic commissioner may also determine that a driver may only drive a PCV as a provisional category D licence holder until he passes a category D re-test.

Production of licence

A licence must be produced on demand to a police officer or, in default, within seven days at a police station nominated by the driver.

Endorsement and disqualification

A disqualification by the courts from holding a category B licence will automatically disqualify the holder from driving a category D or D1 vehicle.

A PCV driver disqualified from holding a D or D1 entitlement will not automatically be debarred from holding a category B entitlement.

Unified driving licences do not contain statements of provisional driving licence entitlements or particulars of convictions, penalty points, endorsements and disqualifications — these are entered on a separate document issued with the licence and known as the counterpart.

Transitional arrangements

The Motor Vehicles (Driving Licences (HGVs and PSVs) Regulations 1990 SI 2611 provide that category D entitlement can be claimed by all existing PSV licence holders.

Holders of Class 1 (double deck PSVs) and Class 2 (large single deck PSVs) licences can claim category D+E entitlement.

Holders of Class 3 (single deck PSVs exceeding 5.5m but not exceeding 8.5m) can claim category D entitlement.

Holders of Class 4A (single deck PSVs not exceeding 5.5m) can claim category D (less than 5.5m) entitlement.

Holders of Class 4B (single deck PSVs not exceeding 5.5m. but restricted to uses specified in the licence) must take a PCV driving test to be able to claim category D entitlement (DVLC Factsheet 4.8.90).

Holders of full HGV driver licences or drivers with full category C (LGV) entitlement can drive PCVs with 17 or more seats if these are not being used for hire and reward and not more than eight passengers are carried.

Fitters and other staff of PSV operators may, if they hold a PCV licence, drive a Large Goods Vehicle up to 10.2 tonnes ULW owned by their employer on his business.

Preserved or historic buses, defined as buses more than 30 years old, may be driven by the holder of a category B licence provided he is age 21 or over, not carrying more than eight passengers and the vehicle is not being used for hire and reward.

Category B entitlement presently includes also Category D1 — minibus not used for hire and reward. These will in the main be Permit minibuses and personnel carriers. It is likely that a further, at present in draft form, EC directive, will require new drivers who obtain their first licence after it is implemented, to take a new PCV category D1 test.

Grandfather rights

Holders of ordinary driving licences or unified licences giving category B + D1 entitlement who had been in the habit of driving PCVs regularly within the last three years could apply before 31.9.92 for a Restricted category D entitlement. This restricted entitlement allows holders to continue to drive large PCVs provided these are not used for hire and reward.

Preparation for the test

Applicants should study:
  (a) the Highway Code
  (b) DOT Pamphlets DL68 — Your Driving Test
  (c) *Driving* — The DOT manual from HMSO and most bookshops.

They should also make sure they know the rules regarding:
  (a) equipment which must by law be carried on a PSV
  (b) conduct of drivers and passengers
  (c) drivers' hours and records regulations
  (d) drivers' responsibilities after an accident.

Applicants should also have a working knowledge of the construction and main component parts of the vehicle, its weight, height, width and length. They should make sure it is roadworthy, has sufficient fuel for the test, displays L plates front and rear, has a road tax disc and a secure seat for the examiner. Applicants must bring their full driving licence and provisional PCV driving licence with them and be punctual.

Working knowledge of the vehicle is an EC requirement which is now a formal part of the test (it has always been tested informally). Applicants are required to understand enough to appreciate when it is unsafe to drive, to be alert to possible defects, and to be able to report verbally or in writing to a fitter or mechanic the repairs thought to be needed.

A driver may drive a PCV immediately on the strength of a pass certificate and the provisional entitlement.

Offences

A person who drives a passenger carrying vehicle on the road without being in possession of the appropriate entitlement commits an offence. Also an employer who employs a person for this purpose can be prosecuted. In both cases a fine on summary conviction can be imposed.

CONDITION OF VEHICLES

CONSTRUCTION AND USE REGULATIONS

The Motor Vehicles (Construction and Use) Regulations 1986 (SI 1986 No. 1078) apply to all motor vehicles, both goods and passenger. Different types of vehicle are defined in the regulations, as listed below.

Definitions

Motor vehicle A mechanically propelled vehicle intended or adapted for use on the roads.

Motor car and heavy motor car A motor car is a mechanically propelled vehicle (excluding a motorcycle or invalid carriage) constructed to carry a load or passengers.

If the vehicle is a passenger vehicle it will be classed as a motor car if its unladen weight does not exceed 3050kg and it is adapted to carry not more than seven passengers.

A *heavy motor car* is a vehicle constructed to carry a load of passengers and exceeds 2540kg unladen weight.

Bus A motor vehicle constructed or adapted to carry nine or more passengers.

Articulated bus A bus so constructed that it can be divided (but only by using workshop facilities) into two vehicles, one of which is a motor vehicle and passengers can at all times pass from one part to another.

Large bus A vehicle constructed or adapted to carry 17 or more seated passengers in addition to the driver.

Coach A large bus with a maximum gross weight of more than 7.5 tonnes and a maximum speed exceeding 60 mph.

Inter-urban motor coach* A vehicle designed and equipped for inter-urban transport having no spaces specifically

---

* *definition contained in the Motor Vehicles (Type Approval for Goods Vehicles (Great Britain) (Amendment) (No.2) Regulations 1991 (SI 1991 No. 1970)).*

intended for standing passengers, but able to carry for short distances passengers standing in the gangway.

Long distance touring coach* A vehicle designed and equipped for long distance journeys, arranged to ensure the comfort of its seated passengers, and which does not carry any standing passengers.

Minibus A motor vehicle constructed or adapted to carry between nine and 16 passengers.

Trailer A vehicle drawn by a motor vehicle but excluding any part of an articulated bus.

Close-coupled In relation to a trailer this means that the wheels on each side remain parallel to the longitudinal axis of the trailer when in motion and the centre of their respective areas of contact with the road does not exceed 1m.

Dual-purpose vehicle A vehicle constructed or adapted for the carriage both of passengers and of goods or burden of any description, with an unladen weight not exceeding 2040kg and which either is four wheel driven or meets the following requirements as to body construction:
  (a) it must have a permanently fitted rigid roof, with or without a sliding panel
  (b) the area to the rear of the driver's seat must:
     (i) be permanently fitted with at least one row of upholstered transverse seats (fixed or folding) for two or more passengers, and
     (ii) have windows, of either glass or other transparent material, at side and rear. The area or aggregate area of light on each side must be not less than 1850cm^2 and at the rear not less than 770cm^2
  (c) the distance between the rearmost part of the steering wheel and the back rests of the row of transverse seats satisfying the requirements specified under (b)(i) above (or, if there is more than one such row of seats, the distance to the rearmost such row) must, when the seats are ready for use, be not less than one-third of

---

* *definition contained in the Motor Vehicles (Type Approval for Goods Vehicles (Great Britain) (Amendment) (No.2) Regulations 1991 (SI 1991 No. 1970)).*

the distance between the rearmost part of the steering wheel and the rearmost part of the floor of the vehicle.

First used Any provision applicable to a motor vehicle first used on or after a specified date need not apply to that vehicle if it was manufactured at least six months before the date.

Maximum weights and dimensions

The maximum weight of a bus with two axles is 17t (17,000kg). If the bus has more than two axles its maximum weight is 24,390kg. This includes water, oil and fuel and an allowance of 65kg per passenger (63.5kg in the case of an articulated bus) and up to four standees. A further allowance per passenger of up to 10kg of luggage is made.

Three axle buses fitted with "road friendly suspension" may gross 25,000kg. Articulated buses may gross 27,000kg maximum.

It is most important that a vehicle does not exceed its maximum gross weight which, if it does, is an absolute offence. If the authorities find a vehicle on the road overweight a prosecution will almost always follow and this can result in both the driver and the operator being heavily fined.

The problems of overweight can occur in a number of ways, eg badly stowed luggage, passengers on trips to the continent taking advantage of lower priced goods such as wines, beers and spirits and "stocking up" before making the return trip, etc.

Whilst the operator should advise passengers of the constraints on the amount of baggage they can carry, the driver should also remind them of these limits, especially in the second example given above, as any surplus may have to be jettisoned if the police or an examiner from the Vehicle Inspectorate (VI) decide to check weigh the vehicle. If the coach is found overweight the police, etc, will require the excess to be off loaded before allowing it to proceed.

Maximum dimensions of buses

Maximum length overall: 12m. However, if the vehicle is a
  minibus, ie a small bus operating under a permit or a
  Community Bus, the maximum length overall is 7m.

Maximum length of a bus and trailer combination: 15m
Maximum length of an articulated bus: 18m
Maximum height: 4.57m
Maximum width: 2.5m

Manufacturer's plates

Every bus, including articulated buses, first used on or after 1.4.82 must be fitted with a manufacturer's plate containing the following particulars:
- manufacturer's name
- vehicle type
- engine type and power
- chassis or serial number
- number of axles
- maximum axle weight for each axle
- maximum gross weight
- maximum train weight
- maximum weight in Great Britain for each axle
- maximum gross weight in Great Britain.

Twin wheels

Twin wheels are regarded as one wheel if their centres of contact with the road are less than 460mm apart.

Speedometers

These must be fitted to all motor vehicles registered from 1.10.37. Requirements for accuracy apply to speedometers incorporated in tachographs, which are required to operate within certain tolerances.

Vehicles first used from 1.4.84 must be fitted with an instrument which allows the speed indication to be read in both mph or kph either simultaneously or, by the operation of a switch, separately.

Vehicles limited by either law or their construction to a speed not exceeding 25mph do not require speedometers.

Speedometers must be maintained in good working order at all "material times", ie when a vehicle is used on a journey unless:
  (a) a defect occurs during a journey, or
  (b) following a defect steps are taken to have the equipment repaired or replaced as soon as possible.

Drivers should report any vehicle where the speedometer is:
(a) not fitted
(b) inoperative
(c) not illuminated
(d) not visible to the driver, or
(e) where it has a broken or missing dial glass.

The requirement to fit speedometers does not extend to vehicles fitted with EC-approved recording equipment, ie tachographs, as such instruments include speedometers.

Speed limiters
Every coach first used from 1.4.74 must be fitted with a speed limiter if it would otherwise be capable of exceeding 70mph.

Speed limiters must be sealed to prevent their being tampered with and the vehicle must display a plate in a conspicuous and readily accessible position reading "SPEED LIMITER FITTED".

Tachographs
In accordance with EC regulations tachographs should be fitted to all vehicles adapted or constructed to carry more than 17 persons, (nine persons if the vehicle is used on international journeys) including the driver. (For more detailed information on tachographs see page 90.)

Television sets
Television receiving apparatus may not be installed in a motor vehicle if the screen is partly or wholly visible to the driver (either directly or reflected) whilst driving the vehicle, unless it is used to display information:
(a) about the state of the vehicle or its equipment
(b) about the location of the vehicle on the road
(c) to assist the driver in seeing the road adjacent to the vehicle
(d) to assist the driver in reaching the destination.

NB: (b) and (c) taken together effectively legalise closed circuit TV reversing devices.

Receiving monitors and videos "Television receiving apparatus" is defined as a cathode ray tube on which can be displayed an image derived from a television broadcast, a recording, camera or computer.

Performing rights If recorded music equipment is installed in a coach (either radio, television or video) a licence must be obtained from the Performing Rights Society, 29/33 Berners Street, London W1 (tel: 071-580 5544).

A fee is payable in respect of each coach with equipment installed (equipment can be transferred between coaches).

Licences are renewable on 6 July each year and fees are raised each January.

Mirrors

All passenger and dual-purpose vehicles must have at least three rear view mirrors, two fitted externally — one on the offside and the other on the nearside — and the third internally (unless a mirror so fitted would be inadequate) to show traffic to the rear and both sides rearwards. On all vehicles registered from 1.4.69 the edges of the internal mirror must be covered by a protective material.

On all vehicles registered after 1.6.78 both the offside mirror and internal mirror must be capable of adjustment from the driving seat.

Each exterior rear view mirror must be visible to the driver either through a side window or through the part of the windscreen swept by the wiper. Drivers should ensure that their mirrors are always clean and correctly positioned to give immediate viewing from the driving position.

All minibuses first used from 1.4.88 must be fitted with rear view mirrors or other means (for example where a rear door is used as a service door, a rear view lens) to enable a seated driver to see the area immediately outside a service door. This requirement is deemed to be met if a driver can see a child 1.3m high standing 1m behind his vehicle.

Safety glass

Passenger and dual-purpose vehicles first used on or after 1.1.59 must have safety glass fitted to the windscreen and all windows on the outside of the vehicle.

The safety glass fitted to the windscreen and all windows wholly or partly in front of and on either side of the driver's seat of motor vehicles manufactured from 1.12.77 and first used from 1.6.78 must conform to specifications BSS857 or BSS5282. The "safety glass" fitted to other windows of a bus (including minibuses) may be *safety glazing* provided that the windows do not:

(a) face the rear of the vehicle and
(b) form the whole or part of a door giving access to the exterior of the vehicle.

Partitions (ie transverse glass windows or panels) not made of safety glass are permissible provided that they are adequately protected against the likelihood of breakage by passengers being thrown against them.

Whilst safety glass is desirable for windows on the upper deck of PCVs, it is mandatory for vehicles manufactured on or after 1.10.81.

Windscreens and windows should be kept clean to ensure a clear view of the road and other traffic.

Windscreen wipers and washers

An efficient automatic windscreen wiper or wipers must be fitted to every vehicle from which an adequate view to the front cannot be obtained other than through the windscreen.

Wipers must be capable of ensuring the driver an adequate view of the road to the front and the front of the near and offsides. Such vehicles, unless they are being used to provide a local service or on a journey incidental to such use, must also be fitted with a windscreen washer which, in conjunction with the wiper, can keep the screen clear of mud, etc.

Horns and reversing alarms

Every motor vehicle must be fitted with an instrument capable of giving audible and sufficient warning of its approach or position. Only a vehicle used on official emergency services may be fitted with a gong, bell siren, two-tone horn or instrument capable of emitting a similar sound.

A reversing alarm may be fitted to a large passenger carrying vehicle having eight or more seats in addition to the driver, provided the sound emitted by the alarm is different to that which is employed at "pelican" pedestrian crossings.

A horn must not be sounded when the vehicle is stationary on a road nor when it is in motion on a restricted road at night between the hours of 23.30 and 07.00, except in an emergency. It may be sounded on a stationary vehicle:
(a) to warn of the presence to or of another moving vehicle on or near the road
(b) to raise the alarm as to theft of the vehicle or its contents

(c) on a PSV to summon assistance for the driver, conductor or inspector.

A reversing alarm fitted to a bus may not be used when the vehicle is on a restricted road between the hours of 23.30 and 07.00

Fuel tanks

Motor vehicle fuel tanks must be so maintained that they are reasonably secure against damage and are free from leakages. Motor vehicles first used from 1.7.73 must be equipped with metal fuel tanks reasonably secured against damage and free from leakages. The requirement does not apply where the vehicle is legibly and indelibly marked with a designated approval mark indicating that the vehicle has been approved in respect of fire risks.

Radio interference suppression

Petrol engined vehicles first used from 1.4.74 must be fitted with radio interference suppression equipment and be clearly marked with the designated approval mark for this equipment.

Smoke

Every motor vehicle must be so constructed that no avoidable smoke or visible vapour is emitted. Excess fuel devices must not be used on diesel engine vehicles whilst in action.

It is an offence to drive a vehicle which is emitting smoke or dangerous vapour.

Tyres

It is illegal to use a tyre:
  (a) which is not correctly inflated
  (b) which has a break in its fabric or a cut in excess of 25mm or 10% of the section width of the tyres, deep enough to reach the body cords
  (c) which has a lump, bulge or tear caused by separation, etc
  (d) which is the wrong size or type for the vehicle's use
  (e) which has any portion of ply or cord exposed
  (f) on which the base of any groove which showed in the original tread pattern is not clearly visible

(g) on which either (i) the grooves of the tread pattern do not have a depth of at least 1mm throughout a continuous band measuring at least ¾ of the breadth of tread and round the entire outer circumference of the tyre, or (ii) where the original tread pattern did not extend beyond ¾ of the breadth of the tread, the base of any groove which showed in the tyre's original tread pattern does not have a depth of at least 1mm.

Note: the grooves of the tread pattern of tyres fitted to passenger vehicles with up to nine seats, goods vehicles not exceeding 3500kg maximum gross weight and light trailers, must be a minimum of 1.6mm in depth throughout a continuous band situated in the central three quarters of the breadth of tread and round the entire outer circumference of the tyre.

"Breadth of tread" means the breadth of that part of the tyre which is in contact with the road under normal conditions of use measured at 90° to the peripheral line of the tread.

"Tread pattern" means the combination of plain surfaces and grooves extending across the breadth of the tread and round the entire outer circumference of the tyres excluding:

    (i) any tie-bars or tread wear indicators
    (ii) any features which are designed to wear out substantially before the rest of the pattern under normal conditions of use and
    (iii) any other minor features.

"Tie-bars" means any part of the tyre moulded in the tread pattern of the tyre for the puprose of bracing two or more features of such tread pattern.

"Tread wear indicators" means any bar, not being a tie-bar, projecting from the base of the tread pattern and moulded between two or more features of the tyre's tread pattern for the purpose of indicating the extent of wear of such a tread pattern.

Points (b), (c) and (e) above do not apply where the tyre and wheel to which it is fitted are so constructed that when running deflated the tyre will operate safely and its outside wall bears an identifying mark to that effect.

These regulations do not apply to a broken down vehicle or a vehicle being taken to a place to be broken up where in either case it is being towed by a vehicle not exceeding 20mph.

Passenger vehicles seating up to eight persons *but not*

buses, may carry specially compact temporary spare wheels/tyres provided that when used the speed of the vehicle does not exceed 50mph.

Recut pneumatic tyres must not be used if the ply or cord has been cut or exposed by the recutting process or it has been wholly or partially recut in a different pattern to that of the manufacturer's recut tread pattern.

It is also illegal to fit to motor vehicles having only two axles and equipped with one or two single wheels, tyres of different types, ie cross-ply, radial or bias-belted, in the following manners:
- (a) diagonal-ply tyres or bias-belted tyres on the rear axle and radial-ply tyres on the front axle or
- (b) diagonal-ply tyres on the rear axle and bias-belted tyres on the front axle.

This does not apply if wide tyres, other than those used for engineering plant, are fitted.

Also, tyres of different structures must not be fitted to vehicles with:
- (a) more than one steerable axle, or
- (b) more than one driven axle not being a steerable axle.

Maintenance of tyres Although maintenance of tyres, like total vehicle maintenance is the responsibility of the maintenance staff, there are certain periodical checks that are the responsibility of the driver.

The following daily check-list is therefore recommended:
- (a) check tyre pressures (cold). Tyres generate heat during running and more so during hot weather, which may cause pressures to rise some 10–15 pounds above the recommended pressure
- (b) examine tyres for cuts, blisters and stones, etc, especially between twin tyres. At first sight any of these may not appear to be dangerous, but they may become so in the course of a journey
- (c) check twin rear tyres. Inner and outer tyres should have the same diameters and the same pressures. One twin tyre below pressure will cause overloading of the other and an eventual blow-out
- (d) make sure that all tyres show a reasonable amount of tread pattern and that the spare wheel and tyre are in similar good order and inflated to the correct pressure.

Note: It is illegal for tyre suppliers to sell car tyres unless the tyre has an "E" marking which shows compliance with load and speed requirements of EC Regulation 30. Also, *retreaded* car and lorry tyres are now illegal unless manufactured and marked in accordance with BS AU 144b: 1977. Drivers should ask a supplier to point out the marking on the tyre if they have to obtain a replacement whilst out on the road.

Tyre service and supply For the benefit of operators or owner-drivers, the tyre manufacturers and their distributors offer substantial repair and replacement facilities. This information is available in booklet form issued free by the distributors and supervised by the National Tyre Distributors Association, Broadway House, The Broadway, London SW19.

This booklet lists over 1100 depots of which around 700 offer a 24 hour service seven days a week.

A copy of the booklet should be among the documents which are always carried on the vehicle.

Tyre loads and speed ratings Vehicles must be fitted with tyres designed to support their maximum axle weights when driven at their maximum permitted speed.

A bus used to provide a local bus service must be fitted with tyres designed to support up to 110% of its maximum weight when driven at 50mph.

Doors
It is an offence to open the door of a vehicle when this may cause injury or damage to any person.

Seat belts and anchorage points
All cars, passenger or dual-purpose vehicles constructed to carry 12 or fewer people (excluding the driver) minibuses of 3500kgs or less first used on or after 1.10.88 and certain light goods vehicles, depending on their registration date and their weight, must be provided with seat belts and anchorage points for the driver's seat and one specified front passenger seat, eg the seat next to the driver or, if the vehicle has more than one front passenger seat, the seat furthest from the driver. Seat

belts and anchorage points are required for all front passenger seats of minibuses. Electrically propelled vehicles are exempt from this requirement.

All cars, passenger and dual-purpose vehicles with seats for eight or fewer passengers (ie buses are excluded) first used on or after 1.4.87 and minibuses first used on or after 1.10.88 must be fitted with a seat belt for any forward facing seat besides the driver's seat, which is not a "specified" (see above) passenger seat.

The fitting of seats with integral seat belts, anchorage points and built-in seat belts is allowed as an alternative to conventional seat belt anchorage points and seat belts.

Vehicles first used from 1.4.73 must be fitted with seat belts which can be put on with one hand and which must be easy to adjust and stow. The stowing device must prevent the belt from lying on the floor.

Seat belts *and* anchorage points must be maintained in a proper condition at all times so that the belt, its anchorages, fastenings and adjusting device are free from any obvious defects which would seriously affect the proper functioning of the seat belt in the event of an accident. Anchorage points and all load bearing parts of the vehicle's structure or panelling within 30cm of each anchorage point must at all times be free from serious corrosion, distortion or fracture.

All passenger vehicles with nine or fewer seats, including the driver's, must have seat belt anchorage points which comply with EC requirements for every forward facing seat.

Drivers are recommended to check the state of their seat belts regularly, not to carry anyone younger than 14 in front and to put notices in their vehicles reminding drivers and passengers to "belt up".

Rear seat belts Cars and dual-purpose vehicles first used on or after 1.1.87 must be fitted with rear seat belts as follows:
 (a) vehicles with not more than two forward facing seats behind the driver's seat:
   (i) an inertia reel belt for at least one seat, or
   (ii) a three-point, lap, or disabled person's belt or child restraint for each seat
 (b) vehicles with more than two (ie up to six) forward facing seats behind the driver's seat:

(i) an inertia reel belt for one outboard seat and a three-point, lap or disabled person's belt for at least one other seat, or

(ii) a three-point belt for one seat and either a child restraint or disabled person's belt for at least one other seat. (One of the two seats fitted must be an outboard seat) or

(iii) a three-point, lap or disabled person's belt or child restraint for each of those seats.

Seat belts on coaches Seat belts and anchorage points must also be fitted to any exposed forward facing seats on coaches first used after 1.10.88. These include the centre rear seat (facing the gangway), driver's seat, crew seat (if fitted), forward facing seats alongside the driver or facing the stair well and any other forward facing seat not immediately behind another forward facing seat with a high (at least 1m) back.

Wearing of seat belts Drivers and front seat passengers of cars, light vans and small passenger vehicles must wear an approved lap and diagonal seat belt. If there is a front passenger bench seat only the person in the outermost seat must wear the seat belt. If this seat is empty the person in the middle has to wear whatever seat belt is provided for that seat. Usually this will be fitted to the front nearside seat but if there is none, the passenger will have to move. If there are no seats beside the driver, the person in the first nearside forward facing seat must wear a belt unless there is a fixed partition between them and the empty space beside the driver.

Exemptions from these requirements are given for specific people, including:
(a) the driver when reversing a vehicle
(b) a driving instructor (as defined in the driving licences regulations) whilst supervising a learner driver in a manoeuvre which includes reversing
(c) the holder of a certificate signed by a registered medical practitioner, exempting him or her from wearing seat belts, on medical grounds
(d) a constable protecting or escorting another person
(e) a prison officer protecting or escorting another person
(f) firemen

(g) a taxi driver whilst seeking hire, answering a call for hire, or carrying a passenger for hire, or the driver of a private hire vehicle whilst the vehicle is being used to carry a passenger for hire

(h) a qualified tester who is conducting a person in a driving test and who, by wearing a seat belt, would endanger himself or any other person

(i) a person occupying a seat where the seat belt either does not conform to the Construction and Use Regulations, or has an inertia reel mechanism which is locked because the vehicle is on, or has been on, a steep incline

(j) a person riding in a vehicle under trade plates whilst investigating or remedying a mechanical fault in the vehicle.

It is the responsibility of the individual to wear the seat belt but responsibility rests with the driver when a child under the age of 14 is being carried in the front seat of the vehicle.

Children under the age of 14 carried in the rear seat of any motor car (excluding a taxi) must wear any "available" seat belts.

Fines can be imposed where these regulations are not complied with.

There is no lower age limit for these regulations but if the passenger is under 14 he or she will not be allowed in the middle front passenger seat without an approved seat belt (it is illegal to carry an unrestrained child in the front seat of virtually any vehicle). Children over one year old may use an adult seat belt or other approved device, unless they are disabled, when they may use any specially designed and constructed seat belt. Disabled adults must use a standard seat belt unless they are in a specially constructed or adapted vehicle, when they may use any seat belt specially designed for them.

NB With the introduction of new regulations in February 1993 where seat belts are fitted to seats in **any** vehicle belts must be worn by persons occupying those seats.

Trailers

Maximum laden weights The maximum laden weight of a trailer manufactured before 27.2.77, with only a parking brake and brakes which operate automatically on overrun of the trailer is 3560kg. For trailers manufactured from 27.2.77 with brakes that operate automatically on overrun and irrespective of any other brakes, the maximum laden weight is 3500kg.

The laden weight of an unbraked trailer used on the road must not exceed its maximum gross weight. It may only be towed by a vehicle whose kerbside weight is at least double the unladen weight of the trailer together with the weight of any load the trailer is carrying.

Trailers under 750kg gross weight must be fitted with brakes if their laden weight exceeds half the towing vehicle's weight.

Unbraked trailers (markings) Every unbraked trailer must be marked in a conspicuous and readily accessible position on the left or nearside with its maximum gross weight (in kg).

Detached trailers When detached from the drawing vehicle a trailer must be prevented from moving by the use of a brake, chain, chock or other efficient device applied to at least one of its wheels.

Length of tow rope Where a motor vehicle is drawing a trailer by means of a tow rope or chain the distance between their nearest points must not exceed 4.5m. Where the distance exceeds 1.5m the tow rope or chain must be made clearly visible from both sides. No limit of length is stated for a rigid tow bar.

Carriage of passengers in trailers No trailer may be used for the conveyance of passengers for hire or reward. Broken down vehicles carrying passengers may be towed provided they are not drawn faster than 30mph and the vehicles are attached by a rigid draw bar.

PSVs drawing trailers Apart from an articulated bus, a bus must not draw a trailer unless:
  (a) it is an empty bus drawing another empty bus which has broken down, or
  (b) it is a trailer with an overall length, including its drawbar, not exceeding 5m *provided* the overall length of the combination does not exceed 18m.

No trailer may, in any circumstances, be drawn by an articulated bus.

Vehicles with rear exits are prohibited from drawing any trailers. Whilst passengers are being carried by a vehicle no person must cause or permit any unnecessary obstruction to any entrance, exit or gangway of the vehicle.

This means that if the vehicle has a rear exit a trailer *must not* be attached.

Brakes

The Construction and Use Regulations lay down specific requirements for the design, application and maintenance of brakes. They do so, in most cases, by applying the requirements of EC Directive 79/486 EC (as most recently amended by Directives 85/647 EC and 676/87 EC). There are further braking requirements specific to PSVs, to be found in the PSV (Conditions of Equipment, Use and Certification) Regulations 1981 (SI 1981 No. 257) (see page 63).

Every passenger vehicle and trailer (except small trailers with total axle weights not exceeding 750kg) first used on or after 1.4.83 must comply with the EC directive. Vehicles first used before that date may also comply with the directive or may comply with the Construction and Use Regulations. There is some slight relaxation in braking criteria for vehicles registered before 1.1.68. If, in addition, the vehicle is a PSV, there are further requirements in the PSV regulations (above) which have to be met.

Parking brake Every passenger vehicle must have a parking brake which is independent of the main brakes and capable, by direct mechanical action, of holding the vehicle stationary on a gradient of at least 16% (ie 1 in 6.25). If the vehicle is required to meet EC braking standards its parking brake must be capable of holding it with an *unbraked* trailer attached on a gradient of 12% (1 in 8.33). A spring brake can be considered to be a mechanical means of action. In the event of a failure of the spring brakes it must be possible to release these without using the normal controls, either pneumatically or manually by a device (eg a spanner) *which must be carried on the vehicle*.

Main and secondary brakes Every passenger vehicle's braking system must have a main means of operation (ie the footbrake) and a secondary means, which could be an emergency brake (often called the "dead man's handle") or a dual system, the "split" part of which is also operated by the footbrake. If one half of the braking system fails the remainder must continue to operate with the required residual efficiency. In the case of a vehicle with a dual braking system the parking brake must be able to operate with the vehicle in motion unless it is a transmission brake.

Retarders Use may be made of a retarder to assist a vehicle to comply with EC braking specifications on downhill speed control and brake fade (with which all vehicles first used before 1.4.90 must comply), but no account may be taken of the contribution of the retarder to assist in complying with the braking efficiencies referred to below.

Certain retarders fitted to buses do not have to meet the anti-lock and braking distribution requirements in EC Directive 85/647.

Braking efficiencies The general minimum braking efficiencies for vehicles to which the regulations apply are as follows:

	Minimum Braking Efficiencies (%)		
	Parking brake	Main brake	Secondary brake
1. Passenger vehicles complying with the EC directive and first used on or after 1.4.83			
drawing an unbraked trailer	12	45	25
2. Passenger vehicles with an independent parking brake first used before 1.4.83 and complying with Construction and Use Regulations	16	50	25
drawing a trailer	16	40	15

Application of trailer brakes The driver must be able to operate the brakes of both the motor vehicle and its trailer, except where the trailer is fitted with an overrun brake, or the trailer is a broken down vehicle being towed in such a manner that it cannot be steered by its own steering gear.

Turning circles and cut out

Buses and minibuses first used from 1.4.82 must be able to turn on either lock so that no part of it projects outside a 12m radius circle or inside a 5.3m radius circle. See diagrams below.

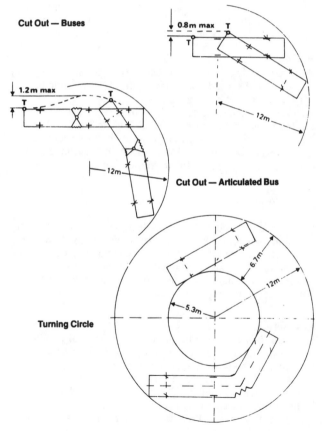

Cut out (swept circle) The side of the vehicle opposite to the direction of turn must not swing out by more than:
   (a) 0.8m (rigid vehicle) or
   (b) 1.2m (articulated vehicle).

Articulated buses
When moving in a straight line the centre of each section must form a continuous line without deflection.

Roof strength of coaches
All new single deck "high floor" (ie with below deck luggage lockers) coaches first used on or after 1.4.93 must comply with ECE Regulation 66 requiring sufficient roof strength to provide a passenger survival space in a "roll-over" accident.

Noise
No motor vehicle or trailer which causes excessive noise may be used on the road, nor may it be used in a manner to cause excessive noise which could be avoided.

Noise or excessive noise emitted by a vehicle includes that emitted by an inefficient exhaust silencer device.

For the purpose of testing and inspection of vehicles on noise limits, levels are laid down in the Construction and Use Regulations which apply EC maximum limits.

LIGHTING

Between sunset and sunrise all vehicles are required to carry two lamps showing white to the front, two lamps showing red to the rear, two red "reflex" reflectors, two red stop lamps, a rear registration plate lamp and direction indicators. Buses also require two headlamps but for those first used before 1.10.69 only one need be a dipped beam lamp.

Restrictions
1. *A red light must not* be shown to the front of a vehicle.
2. *A white light must not* be shown to the rear of a vehicle except in the following circumstances:
   (a) for the purpose of reversing
   (b) in order to illuminate the interior of a vehicle
   (c) to illuminate the rear number plate
   (d) to illuminate a PSV destination board or a taxi meter.

Special provisions do permit the use of blue, amber or green lights on fire, ambulance, or police service vehicles, medical practitioners' vehicles and special service vehicles.

Use of headlamps and auxiliary lamps Headlamps must be used during the hours of darkness in all unlit areas (or where the street lamps are more than 200 yards apart). "Hours of darkness" is usually defined as half an hour after sunset to half an hour before sunrise.

Both lights must be illuminated together and it is an offence to drive in non-illuminated areas (where street lamps are more than 200 yards apart) with only one headlamp working.

Headlamps must be switched off when the vehicle is stationary except at traffic stops. They must not be fitted more than 1200mm from the ground, nor less than 500mm from the ground.

Headlamps must be fitted with a dipping mechanism to avoid dazzle and no light other than a dipping headlight may be moved, by swivelling or otherwise, while the vehicle is in motion. Every matched pair of headlamps must emit beams of the same colour light. Lamps fitted and used as fog or spotlights must be fitted with a permanently deflected beam. There is no minimum height for these lamps provided they are used only during poor visibility.

Road clearance vehicles and large passenger carrying vehicles first used before 1.10.69 are permitted to use only one headlamp. A vehicle being towed and a snow plough are exempt from using headlamps.

Front fog lamps

In conditions where visibility is seriously reduced, two fog lamps or a fog lamp and a spot lamp may be used instead of headlamps.

Fog lamps may emit either a white or yellow light and must be positioned so that they do not dazzle or cause inconvenience to other road users.

High intensity rear fog lamps

Rear fog lamps must be fitted to vehicles and trailers first used from 1.4.80. Either a single or a matched pair of rear fog lamps can be fitted.

Rear fog lamps may only be used in conditions of poor visibility and must be switched *off* as soon as conditions improve. They may *not* be wired through to the vehicle's brake light circuit.

Direction indicators

All vehicles must be fitted with direction indicators. Indicators can be of the flashing or semaphore type but the latter may only be fitted to vehicles registered before September 1965. Indicators on vehicles first used from September 1965 must show amber both to the front and rear. They must flash at a rate of between 60 and 120 flashes per minute.

Emergency and other services' vehicles

Distinctive lamps emitting blue, amber or green flashing lights are permitted on certain vehicles carrying out emergency or other services.

Ambulances, fire engines, fire salvage vehicles, Forestry Commission or local authority vehicles used for fire fighting, police vehicles, blood transfusion service vehicles, bomb disposal, RAF mountain rescue vehicles, HM coastguard or coastguard auxiliary vehicles used for emergencies on or near the coast, NCB mine rescue vehicles, RNLI vehicles used for launching lifeboats and vehicles used for carrying human tissue for transplants, etc, are permitted to carry one or more *blue* lamps.

Vehicles used for road clearance; for testing, maintaining, improving, cleansing or watering roads; inspecting, renewing or installing any apparatus in, on, under or over a road; vehicles constructed or adapted for refuse collection; vehicles having a maximum speed not exceeding 25mph; vehicles having an overall width exceeding 2.9m; breakdown vehicles; vehicles authorised by an Order under s.44 of the Road Traffic Act 1988, ie special type vehicles or trailers constructed for special purposes, etc and vehicles used by HM Customs and Excise for testing fuels, are permitted to carry one or more *amber* lights.

Vehicles used by registered medical practitioners registered by the General Medical Council may carry one or more *green* lamps when used in an emergency.

Warning beacons fitted to vehicles used at airports may emit a *yellow* light.

All such lamps must be fitted so that the centre is at least *1200mm* above the ground and be visible from any point at a reasonable distance from the vehicle. The frequency of the flashing from these lamps must not be less than 60 nor more than 240 equal times per minute and the interval between each flashing must be constant.

The lamps may only be used when the vehicle is being used for the relevant purposes and in the case of a breakdown vehicle the amber lights may only be illuminated when the vehicle is being used in connection with, or near to, an accident or breakdown, or towing a disabled vehicle. Such vehicles are permitted an additional white lamp for illuminating the area of the accident or breakdown but it must be directed so as not to dazzle or inconvenience other road users.

Road clearance vehicles are also permitted to carry an amber reflecting surface to the rear of the vehicle.

Stop lights, reversing lights and trailer lights

Stop lights must be fitted to all vehicles and must always be maintained in a clean and efficient working order.

Reversing lights are not compulsory fittings but if fitted to a vehicle they must be maintained in efficient working order.

Trailer and trailer caravan lighting requirements are the same as those applying to motor vehicles with a few exceptions. Trailers which do not have side lamps *must* have front corner lamps.

Use of hazard warning lights

Hazard warning lights may be used only when the vehicle is stationary on any part of the road, for the purpose of warning other drivers that the vehicle is temporarily causing an obstruction *or* whilst travelling on motorways or unrestricted dual carriageways to warn drivers of following vehicles of the need to slow down because of an obstruction ahead. They may also be used by drivers of buses to summon assistance for the driver, conductor or an inspector on the bus.

Lights required during daylight hours

The law requires vehicles travelling on a road where visibility is seriously reduced to have obligatory lamps switched on, ie side and rear position lamps and either headlamps or a pair of front fog lamps and rear fog lamps.

It should be noted that front and rear fog lamps may *only* be used in conditions where visibility is *seriously reduced* during the day or at night — it is illegal to use them at any other time.

Lights required on stationary vehicles at night

Passenger vehicles, other than buses (ie with seats for more than eight passengers) may be parked at night on a restricted road (ie within a 30mph zone) *without lights* if:

    (a) they are parked with their nearside close to and parallel to the kerb (except when standing in a recognised parking place or on either side of a one way street) *and*

    (b) no part of the vehicle is within *10m* of a road junction.

No lights are required on a vehicle if it is parked within the confines of an area outlined by lamps or traffic signs (cones) to prevent the vehicle etc from being a danger to other road users.

Any vehicle to which a trailer is attached must keep its lights (side lights) on when parked on the road at night.

General requirements

Headlamps, front and rear fog lamps and reversing lamps (if fitted) must be set so that they do not dazzle or cause inconvenience to other road users. It is also a requirement of the law that all lights and reflectors, including hazard warning lights are kept clean and in good working order.

Number plates

Vehicles not exceeding three tons unladen weight, first registered on or after 1.1.73 must be fitted with reflex-reflecting number plates. Only the background may be made of reflex-reflecting material and this must be white for the front plate and yellow for the back plate with letters and figures in black on both.

Vehicles first registered before 1.1.73 may also be fitted with reflex-reflecting number plates as an alternative to the existing type.

A trailer (including a broken-down vehicle being towed) must have the registration number of the towing vehicle fitted on the rear of the vehicle on tow.

VEHICLE CERTIFICATION, APPROVAL, INSPECTION AND ANNUAL TESTING

Whilst manufacturers and operators have the responsibility for the above, brief details are included in this guide since:
(a) owner-drivers will need the information and
(b) employee-drivers should be aware of the requirements of the legislation and be able to check that the vehicles they drive comply.

Certification of Initial Fitness

No PSV which is adapted to carry more than eight passengers may be used unless either:
(a) a certifying officer has issued a *Certificate of Initial Fitness*
(b) a certificate has been issued by the Department of Transport approving the vehicle as a *type vehicle* of a particular type and a certifying officer (if he is satisfied that the vehicle complies with prescribed conditions of fitness) has issued a *Certificate of Conformity*
(c) a *type approval certificate* has been issued.

(Passenger vehicles with over eight seats have not yet come within the scope of type approval and neither have trailers.)

Once in service PSVs must be tested annually on the anniversary of their *first registration* (not their Certificate of Initial Fitness date). Recertification is no longer required but the vehicles are subject to a system of prohibition where necessary.

If (a) or (b) is issued before *registration* it must be sent to the Department of Transport so that the registration number of the vehicle can be noted and the certificate returned.

Vehicle inspections

All motor vehicles, including PSVs, are subject to spot checks, either at the roadside or at an operator's premises.

Authorised police officers and the Department of Transport's Vehicle Inspectorate (VI) examiners may, on production of their authority, test or inspect a vehicle on the road. (Only a police officer in uniform may require a vehicle to stop on the road.) It is an offence to obstruct an authorised examiner, although drivers of motor vehicles which are *not PSVs* may request a deferred test, which may be refused by a police officer if it appears to him or her that:

(a) because of an accident involving the vehicle a test should be immediately conducted, or
(b) the vehicle is so defective that it ought not to be allowed to proceed without first being tested.

If an authorised examiner discovers a defect he or she may, in addition to instituting proceedings for a breach of Construction and Use Regulations, serve a defect notice on the owner via the driver (if this is not the owner) of the vehicle requiring, within 28 days, a certificate from an MOT testing station "clearing" the defect.

An examiner may drive a vehicle in order to test it. An examiner or police officer in uniform may inspect a motor vehicle on premises provided the consent of the owner of the vehicle and/or premises is obtained, or 48 hours' notice of intended inspection is given (72 hours if notice is sent by recorded delivery).

Inspection of PSVs

The rules relating to inspection of PSVs by authorised police officers or Vehicle Inspectorate (VI) examiners are stricter than those given above. They may enter premises to conduct tests at any reasonable time, carry out roadside checks, and if necessary detain vehicles to do so. There is no provision to opt for a delayed test. Drivers must give reasonable assistance to authorised police officers and examiners. Vehicle examiners or police officers in uniform may direct a vehicle which is stationary on a road to be taken to any place not more than five miles distant for inspection purposes. Powers to conduct roadside checks (but not fleet inspections) extend to all buses with more than eight seats, even if these (eg Permit Minibuses and Community Buses) are not PSVs.

Following an inspection as above authorised police officers and vehicle examiners have similar, but not identical powers to prohibit the use of the vehicle. Both may issue an immediate prohibition if they consider the vehicle unfit for service, but only a vehicle examiner may issue a delayed prohibition. Prohibitions relating to passenger vehicles cannot be removed until the vehicle has been inspected in accordance with the directions on the prohibition, which can specify a re-test at an official PSV Testing Station or at an operator's premises if tests are conducted there.

The imposition of a prohibition and the use of a vehicle in contravention of a prohibition can have serious consequences for an operator and may even jeopardise the PSV O licence.

Drivers should immediately report any prohibition received to their employers.

The forms of prohibition in use by the police and VI are:

PG9	Prohibition of driving a vehicle on the road (applicable to ALL vehicles)
PG9/ABC	Combined Refusal/Variation and Exemption
PG9A	Variation of terms of a PG9
PG9B	Permitting the movement of a prohibited vehicle to a place of repair under stated conditions
PG9D	Prohibition/variation defect continuation sheet
PG10	Removal of a prohibition
PGDN	Defect notice (where the defect does not warrant prohibition).

Drivers (or their employers) are also legally bound to report to the Traffic Commissioner any damage or accident to a PSV which might affect the safety of its operation.

Weighing of buses etc

Persons authorized by a Highway Authority, or police constable authorized in writing by a Police Authority or a Chief Officer of Police, may require a person in charge of a bus etc, to allow it or any trailer drawn by it to be weighed or to proceed to a weighbridge for that purpose.

Only a police officer in uniform can stop a moving vehicle.

There is no provision for authorized persons to require the bus etc, to be unloaded to ascertain unladen weight.

If, when the vehicle is weighed, it appears to either an authorized person (ie a Trading Standards officer or police constable) or vehicle examiner that the Construction and Use limits as to the weight of the vehicle have been exceeded or that by reasons of excess overall weight or excess axle weight the driving of the vehicle would involve danger or injury to any person, any of the above persons may serve a notice in writing prohibiting the driving of the vehicle on the road until —

- the weight has been reduced, and
- official notice has been given to the person in charge of the vehicle that it is permitted to proceed.

Removal of a prohibition may be withheld until the vehicle has been re-weighed.

The authorized persons or vehicle examiner may also give a direction in writing requiring the removal of the vehicle to a specified place (up to 5 miles distant) subject to any conditions in the direction and driving the vehicle under such a direction whilst overweight will not be an offence.

Vehicle testing

Tests of passenger vehicles, including most PSVs and taxis are carried out annually after their first examination (which is usually conducted on or before the first anniversary of their registration).

The only exception to this rule is the *three year Class IV MOT test* which applies to passenger vehicles with eight or fewer seats (including such vehicles used as a PSV unless they have a CIF). Also within the scope of the *Class IV MOT test* are passenger vehicles with more than eight but fewer than 13 seats but these have be tested annually after one year. Class IV tests are usually carried out by an authorised examiner (ie private garages franchised for this purpose by the DOT) but may also be carried out by designated councils (ie County or District councils authorised for this purpose by the DOT).

Vehicles with more than 12 passenger seats, including works buses, minibuses used under a Minibus Permit and PSVs which may lawfully be used on a road without a CIF (ie Community Buses and LEA school buses) require a *Class V test*. This is the same as a car MOT test but must be carried out either:

(a) at a DOT LGV testing station or
(b) by a designated council or
(c) by an authorised examiner whose authorisation permits him to test vehicles in this class.

Drivers of such vehicles should check that their "authorised examiner" is permitted to test Class V vehicles. PSVs with more than eight seats and having a CIF and large buses (designed to carry more than 16 passengers, excluding the driver) require a Class VI test which is conducted by a DOT vehicle examiner either at a LGV testing station or at certain designated large operator's premises. This test is more rigorous and comprehensive than the Class IV or V MOT tests and covers every item specified in the *PSV Testers Manual* (available from HMSO).

Summary

As previously stated, tests of passenger vehicles including PSVs and taxis are carried out anually after their first examination which is usually on or before the first anniversary of their registration (but may in a few cases be on or before their third anniversary). They may be carried out by DOT vehicle examiners, examiners authorised by the DOT to inspect vehicles or designated councils. The table below shows, by seating capacity, the class of test to which various vehicles are subject, and by whom they are to be examined.

Class	Non PSVs	PSVs	First examination after	Examined by		
				DOT	Authorised Examiner	Designated council
IV	eight or fewer seats*	eight or fewer seats	three years	×	✓	✓
	more than eight but 12 or fewer seats*		one year	×	✓	✓
V	more than 12 seats* including work buses and "Permit" minibuses	PSVs which can be used without CIF, ie Community Buses, LEA's school buses	one year	✓	ø	✓
VI		PSVs with more than eight seats not in Class V	one year	✓	—	—

ø Only a few authorised examiners have the facilities to test Class V vehicles and are authorised to so so.
× There is a public Department of Transport testing facility at Hendon.
* Excluding the driver's seat.

FITNESS, EQUIPMENT AND USE OF PSVs AND MINIBUSES

PSV CONDITIONS OF FITNESS

The PSV (Conditions of Fitness, Equipment, Use and Certification) Regulations 1981 (SI 1981 No. 257) are the major source of legislation covering the design of PSVs. Similar regulations apply to minibuses with between nine and 16 seats (excluding the driver's seat) used under ss.18-21 of the Transport Act 1985 (Permit minibuses and Community Buses). These regulations place no less emphasis on safety but relax or omit many of the "comfort" requirements (eg seat spacing or headroom). Minibuses may now comply with further relaxed criteria in Schedules 6 and 7 of the Road Vehicle (Construction and Use) Regulations 1986 (SI 1986 No. 1078).

Many of the requirements of the regulations do not apply to vintage vehicles.

The main provisions of the PSV (Conditions of Fitness Equipment Use and Certification) Regulations 1981 (SI 1981 No. 257) likely to be of interest to drivers are detailed below.

Stability

PSVs are "tilt tested" at their first test for a Certificate of Initial Fitness. During the test the vehicle must not overturn before the surface on which it stands has reached the following angles from the horizontal:

Single deck fully laden	Tilt angle 35°
Double deck top deck fully laden	Tilt angle 28°

For the test the vehicles must be loaded as shown overleaf with weights of 63.5kg (representing a load of average passengers, driver, and, if carried, conductor).

Drivers should take great care where luggage is stowed on roof racks. It is advisable to try and prevent large numbers of school children congregating on the top deck of double deck vehicles if the lower saloon is unoccupied.

Guard rails or body "skirts" between the front and rear wheels of a PSV must extend to within 310mm (12" approx) of the ground, 155mm (6" approx) from the rear wheel and 230mm (9" approx) from the front wheel when the vehicle is unladen, with no passengers and standing on level ground.

Tilt Testing of PSVs

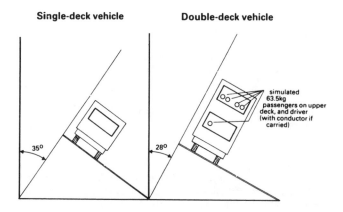

Guard Rails

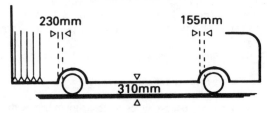

Drivers should check periodically for any missing or insecure guard rails.

Brakes

The EC Braking Regulations now apply to all passenger vehicles with eight or fewer seats, buses first used before 1.4.83 if they have a manufacturer's Certificate of Conformity certifying that they conform to EC Regulations as a "type vehicle" and buses first used after 1.4.83.

There are additional requirements for PSVs which are not "type approved".

1. All the brakes of a PSV must act directly on the wheels of the vehicle and not through the transmission. (Transmission brakes are only allowed on PSVs registered before 1.1.55.)

2. An exception is made for mechanically operated brakes which work without the intervention of any stored energy if:
   (a) there is no universal joint between the brake and the wheel
   (b) failure of any part of the mechanism would not cause the wheel to become detached, and
   (c) all the wheels of the vehicle are fitted with brakes operated by the same means.
3. The brakes of one of the braking systems must be operated by a pedal.

Fuel tanks

On half deck vehicles, lower decks of double deck vehicles and single deck vehicles with seats for more than 12 passengers, fuel tanks may not be positioned under gangways or within 600mm of a primary emergency exit, or anywhere in the driver or passenger compartments.

On single deck passenger vehicles carrying not more than 12 passengers the fuel tank may not be placed under or within 300mm of any exit and the filling point must not be at the rear.

Fuel tanks must only be able to be filled from outside the vehicle.

There must be a fuel cut off device accessible from outside the vehicle:
   (a) on diesel engined vehicles it need not be immediately visible so long as its position is clearly marked on the outside of the vehicle and the means of operation is clearly indicated
   (b) on petrol engined vehicles it must be visible and the "off" position must be marked.

(Some smaller vehicles are fitted with dashboard mounted emergency engine stops/fuel cut offs, often operated by means of the ignition key. Provided the key when turned to off stops the engine, and that the location and means of operation is correctly marked, this is not a reason for rejection when the vehicle is submitted for annual testing.)

The maintenance of fuel tanks is most important. Drivers should immediately report any insecure, leaking or corroded fuel tank or vehicles without a filler cap or with one of a type which does not prevent spillage.

Silencers and noise

Every vehicle fitted with an internal combustion engine must be fitted with an exhaust system including a silencer. They must be maintained in good and efficient working order.

Exhaust gases must not escape into the atmosphere without first passing through the silencer fitted to the vehicle.

Vehicles are subject to spot checks on the road to ensure that they do not make more noise than the standards allow.

All vehicles registered after 1.4.70 must meet stringent limits on noise. Vehicles manufactured from 1.4.83 and first used from 1.10.83 are subject to even more stringent noise limits in so far as they relate to noise levels *measured on the road*. However, these do not apply to a vehicle proceeding to a place where by previous arrangement noise tests are to be carried out or adjustments, modifications or equipment is to be fitted so that the vehicle complies, or when a vehicle is returning from such a place immediately after the noise has been so tested.

Exhaust pipes

Exhaust pipes must be so fitted or shielded so that there is no likelihood of any flammable material falling on them from any part of the vehicle and so that they are unlikely to cause a fire as a result of proximity to any flammable material on the vehicle.

The outlet should be either at the rear or offside and close enough to the rear to prevent, as far as possible, fumes entering the vehicle.

Drivers should report any exhaust system likely to create a fire or fume hazard, or which is wrongly positioned.

Outlets from ancillaries such as toilet, sink or cooking facilities must be designed to prevent the deposit of waste on the road surface.

Electrical equipment

On vehicles registered on or after 19.6.68 any electrical circuit with a voltage of over 100 volts must be capable of being isolated from the main supply by a dual pole switch (unless one pole of the circuit is earthed).

The switch must not disconnect the obligatory lights required by the Road Vehicles Lighting Regulations 1984.

Body and suspension

The body must be securely fixed to the chassis and every trap door or suspension flap secured so that it cannot become dislodged by vibration. Catches or lifting devices must not project above the floor.

The suspension must prevent any excessive body sway. Failure of any part of the suspension (except tyres) should not cause the driver to lose directional control.

On open top vehicles the side rails or panels must be at least 910mm (1.21m at the front and back) above the top deck and 455mm above the seats.

Luggage racks

These must be constructed so that any article on them, if it becomes dislodged whilst the vehicle is in motion, is unlikely to fall on the driver or affect his control.

Artificial lighting

Adequate internal illumination must be provided on each deck of a PSV (except in the case of an open top double deck) and, on vehicles registered after 1.4.59, on every step or platform providing an entrance or exit (other than an emergency exit).

On double-deck PSVs registered on or after 28.10.64 there must be a dual lighting circuit so that the failure of either sub-circuit does not "black out" either deck.

Steps

The lowest entrance step of an unladen PSV must never be more than 435mm (approximately 17") above ground level. This is the normal entrance step height of a coach body, but on many services operated under a tendered-for subsidy agreement there is a requirement for a lower entrance step. At least one lamp must be provided as near as is practicable to the top of every staircase leading to the top deck of a double deck vehicle.

Drivers should immediately report:
(a) a tread case, step, stairway or platform found to be weak or insecure, or excessively worn, or with inadequate anti-slip covering

(b) a lighting deficiency causing inadequate illumination of step, stairs, platform or interior
(c) lighting circuits not split, so that a failure of one circuit does not leave part illumination on each deck.

Entrances and exits

Every vehicle first used after October 1987 must have a *primary* emergency exit of the height of a standing adult (1.37m) leading directly from the saloon of a single deck bus or the lower deck of a double deck bus directly to the outside of the vehicle. *Secondary* emergency exits are openings of smaller dimensions. Where only two exits are specified there must be one on either side of the vehicle and there must be an emergency exit on the top deck of double deckers.

The regulations relating to the minimum number of exits depend on the vehicle's age and seating capacity.

		Min No. of Exits	
No of Seats	Age of Vehicle	Primary	Secondary
45 or less	Pre 1981	----	2†
	Post 1981	1	1*
Over 45	Pre 1981	2	1
	Post 1981	1	2*

* one must be of no smaller dimensions than a primary exit
† one may also serve as a primary exit.

In addition double-decked coaches first used from 1.4.90 must be fitted with a means of escape in both halves of the vehicle either by the provision of a second staircase or a hammer or other device which can be used to break any side window of the vehicle in case of an emergency. If the latter is to be used it must be displayed in a conspicuous position on the upper deck with an "IN EMERGENCY" sign together with instructions on use nearby.

Note that the main passenger entrance may also qualify as an *exit*.

Every *entrance* of a vehicle must be on the nearside but one or more entrances may be placed on the offside (not counting as exits) provided they are fitted with doors controlled by the driver from his seat with a controlling device which is clearly separate and distinguishable from any device for opening or closing any entrance door on the nearside.

The minimum width of entrances is 530mm.

All *emergency exits* must be clearly *marked* both inside and on the outside if they can be opened therefrom, fitted with forward opening doors and readily accessible to passengers. Emergency exits in single deck vehicles or on the lower decks of double deck vehicles must be situated so that passengers can step directly from the gangway to the outside of the vehicle.

The means of operation of doors fitted to emergency exits (which must *not* be power operated) must be clearly indicated and readily accessible to persons of normal height standing outside the vehicle.

Doors

There must be a means of securing the door closed, ie a catch, on every entrance and exit.

If a door on a vehicle is capable of remaining open whilst the vehicle is in motion, or may be accidentally closed whilst the vehicle is in motion, there must also be a means of securing it open.

Each door must have two devices (ie handles) for operating it:

(a) for normal operation which may be by the vehicle owner or person authorised by him or her and

(b) for operating the door from outside the vehicle.

They must be designed to operate with a single movement of the handle and the means of operation must be clearly indicated.

The direction of any manual effort required to operate must be shown (eg "pull to open") and, if the door is power operated, there must be a statement that it may only be used by passengers in an emergency.

If the door operating device is not placed on the door itself:

(a) it must be placed where it is readily associated with it and

(b) its location must be clearly indicated.

All devices must be capable of being operated by a person of normal height (without risk of being struck by the door where the device is not on the door itself) and be so designed that they cannot be accidentally dislodged.

Every door must operate without obstructing access to any entrance or exit from inside or outside the vehicle.

If a door on a vehicle is *power operated* and projects more than 80mm from the side (excluding any mouldings) when opened it must be *interlocked* with the transmission so that the vehicle cannot move off with the door open (except when operated in an emergency as above).

The operation of the brakes must be in no way adversely affected by the operation of any power operated door. If the power operated system fails, the door must be capable of being opened manually.

On vehicles having power operated doors, if the interlocking between the door operating mechanism and the transmission, referred to above, is absent, the vertical edges of the doors must be fitted with soft rubber.

All vehicles registered on or after 1.4.80 with power operated doors fitted more than 500mm behind the back of the driver's seat must, from 1.4.93, meet three conditions:

1. Automatically re-open if prevented from closing by an object 60mm high (eg a foot)
2. Automatically re-open if fingers or a hand are trapped, unless these can be "readily extracted".
3. Have a "tell tale" light visible to the driver to warn if not fully closed.

Drivers should report immediately if a flap or door has a broken or loose hinge, or is damaged so that it cannot be secured or held open, or has a sharp or protruding edge or defective locking mechanism.

Access to exits

There must be unobstructed access to at least two exits from every seat in a vehicle (unless the fitness regulations require only a single exit).

This requirement need not be met in the case of:
(a) any seat beside the driver's seat, accessible by a single entrance other than the driver's door
(b) a seat on an open top of a double deck vehicle, having unobstructed access to one exit.

A barrier placed at the foot of the staircase on a double deck vehicle to prevent passengers riding upstairs (eg in "off peak" operation) does not prevent the vehicle complying with this regulation.

No seat may be fitted to any door of a PSV.

Drivers should report immediately if the access to an exit or emergency exit is obstructed (or if the means of breaking any windows designated as emergency exits are missing, inadequate or not clearly marked).

Every gangway on a PSV must be at least 305mm wide at deck level, widening further at "hip" and "shoulder" level. Passages of similar width must be provided between gangways and emergency exits and, on vehicles with seats for more than 12 passengers, gangways must be increased in width to 530mm within 910mm of any entrance or exit.

The minimum prescribed heights of gangways in vehicles adapted to carry more than 12 passengers are as follows.

Single deck vehicles and lower decks of double deck vehicles:

with 14 or fewer seats	1.6m
with more than 14 seats	1.77m
top deck of double deck vehicles	1.72m.

The minimum height of gangways on vehicles with seats for 12 or fewer passengers is 1.42m reducing to 1.21m at points within 305mm of any entrance or exit.

Drivers should report a dangerously worn or contaminated gangway or entrance mat.

Seating

The supports of all seats must be securely fixed in position.

Each seat must have a closed back rest designed to prevent passengers' pockets being picked from behind.

The positioning of seats on PSVs is governed by the minimum dimensions shown.

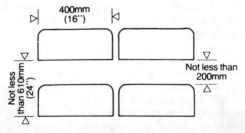

There must be protection, in the form of a guard rail or screen, for seated passengers, where there is any likelihood of their being thrown against an entrance or exit.

The front of any seat must not be any closer than 225mm to any well or step.

Drivers should report:
(a) distorted or fractured seat frames
(b) insecure seating
(c) insecure fittings or arm rests having sharp projections
(d) dirty or damaged seat coverings.

Courier seats Crew seats (as the regulations describe these folding seats) may now be fitted at the front of PSVs.

The requirements for the construction and use of courier/crew seats are that they must be provided with arm rests and a suitable place for the occupant to rest his or her feet. There must be at least 300mm clear space in front of the leading edge of the crew seat and, whether in or out of use, the crew seat must not impede the driver's field of vision. When in use it is permissible for the crew seat to protrude into the gangway but those parts which do protrude must automatically retract when the seat is not in use.

The words "for crew use only" must be marked on or near each crew seat in letters at least 10mm tall.

Driver's accommodation

The driver must have a means of preventing light from the vehicle interior disturbing him or her, and, if the vehicle has more than 12 seats, the driver's seat must be adjustable both vertically and horizontally.

Where access to this seat is from the offside, the means of entry must be at least 455mm wide and provided with a grab handle and step if the entrance is more than 690mm above the ground. If the cab is enclosed there must be an emergency escape window at least 530mm x 455mm other than on the offside.

On all vehicles with more than 12 passenger seats where access to the driver's seat is by means of a passage, the passage must be at least 300mm wide.

Ventilation

This must be adequate for driver and passengers without the need to open a window to demist the windscreen. Drivers should report missing, inoperative or blocked demisting and ventilating equipment.

Windscreens
These must be capable of being opened to give the driver a clear view ahead unless there is an adequate demisting and defrosting device. In practice the demisting requirement is normally met.

Signals A means of signalling the driver to stop must be provided on passenger vehicles with 12 or more seats. Drivers should report any broken or missing system of passenger communication.

EQUIPMENT OF PSVs

Fire extinguishers and first aid
Every PSV must carry a fire extinguisher to British Standard 5423:1977, 1980 or 1987 and every vehicle on non-local services must carry a first aid box suitable for storing the items referred to.

These must be:
(a) readily available for use
(b) clearly marked as a first aid box, or, if a fire extinguisher, with the appropriate BSI specification number
(c) maintained in good order.

The items to be carried in the first aid box, which must be of good and reliable quality and suitable design, are:
(a) 10 antiseptic wipes, foil packed
(b) one conforming disposable bandage (not less than 7.5cm wide)
(c) two triangular bandages
(d) one packet of 24 assorted adhesive dressings
(e) three large sterile unmedicated ambulance dressings (not less than 15cm x 20cm)
(f) two sterile eye pads, with attachments
(g) 12 assorted safety pins
(h) one pair of rustless blunt-ended scissors.

A first aid box which is inaccessible, obviously in poor condition, illegibly marked or missing, and a fire extinguisher which is inaccessible, obviously discharged or missing, should be immediately reported by the driver.

USE OF PSVs

Obstruction of entrances, exits and gangways
No unnecessary obstruction to the above must be caused or permitted whilst passengers are being carried.

Obstruction of driver
No person shall cause or permit any unnecessary obstruction to the driver.

Body maintenance
Vehicles must not be used to carry passengers unless the windows, fittings and seats are in a clean and good condition.

Lamps
If carrying passengers during the hours of darkness, vehicles must have sufficient lights operating to illuminate the access to all seats and exits and any emergency exit markings. This may be extinguished on the upper deck of a double deck vehicle if a barrier is secured at the foot of all stairways.

Power operated doors
Except in an emergency, power operated doors may only be operated by the driver or by some other person authorised by the operator, and then not if the vehicle is in motion.

Filling of petrol tank
While the engine is running the petrol tank filler cap may not be removed or petrol put into the tank.

Carriage of conductors
No vehicle with more than 20 seats may be used on a local service without a conductor unless:
  (a) it is a single deck vehicle with seats for less than 32 passengers and the emergency exit is at the front of the vehicle, visible to the driver and the entrance is also visible so that the driver is aware of any passenger trapped in the door or
  (b) a certifying officer has certified in writing that a conductor is not required.

Carriage of flammable or dangerous substances
In addition to any requirements under petroleum or similar

regulations, flammable or dangerous substances may only be carried if in containers designed and constructed to minimise the risk of damage to the vehicle or injury to passengers in the event of an accident.

Markings

The name and address of the authority, company or individual to whom the PSV "O" licence was issued and their principal place of business must be marked on the vehicle's nearside in a conspicuous position, in clearly legible characters at least 25mm tall, in colours contrasting with their background. Similarly the seating and standing capacity must be marked on the inside.

All emergency exits should be marked both inside and outside the vehicle.

Missing or illegible statutory markings should be reported by the driver.

MINIBUS CONDITIONS OF FITNESS

Minibuses first used on or after 1.4.88 no longer have to meet the former stringent requirements for fitness, equipment and use. These have now been considerably relaxed by the Construction and Use Regulations 1986 (Schedules 6 and 7).

In addition existing minibuses are permitted to comply with these regulations as an optional alternative to complying with the previous and more stringent Minibuses (Conditions of Fitness, Equipment and Use) Regulations 1977 (SI 1977 No. 2103).

Definition

The Construction and Use Regulations define a minibus as having more than eight but not more than 16 seats excluding the driver's seat.

Drivers' responsibility for compliance

Many of the requirements of the schedules relate to the construction of the vehicle and are thus in the main the concern of the manufacturer and the operator but in some cases responsibility for ensuring continuing compliance and reporting defects rests also with the driver.

Doors

Every minibus must have one service door on the nearside plus an emergency door on the rear or at the offside. (An offside driver's door does not constitute an emergency door, but a rear opening service door can do so.)

Every emergency door must be clearly marked in letters at least 25mm high on both the inside and the outside *"Emergency Door"* or *"For Emergency Use Only"*, and its means of operation must be clearly indicated on or near the door. It must open outwards and be capable of being manually operated.

Any power operated doors must have transparent panels enabling a person immediately outside the door to be seen, and be capable of being operated by the driver from his seat. It must also be capable of being opened from both inside and outside the vehicle by the use of over-riding controls (clearly marked so as to indicate their means of operation) on or near the door. The marking must state that these controls can be used by passengers *only* in an emergency.

Power operated doors must have sensitive soft edges which will detect trapped limbs and reverse the closing motion of the door. If such an auto-release system is worked from stored energy it must be designed so as not to adversely affect the operation of the vehicle's brakes.

It must be possible to operate every door from inside the minibus, even if they can be locked from outside. Handles which open doors from the inside must operate with a single movement but must also be designed, so far as is reasonably possible, to prevent accidental opening of the door. Doors must be hinged at the edge nearest the front of the vehicle and either be closed by a two stage slam lock or protected by a "tell tale" device which will warn the driver if the door is opened.

The driver must also, by the use of mirrors or otherwise, be able to clearly see the areas both inside and outside every service door — see also page 39 regarding the driver's view of minibus doors.

There must be unobstructed (except by tilting/folding seats or ramps) access from every passenger seat to at least two doors and a grab handle or hand rail at every side service door to assist passengers boarding or alighting.

Seats
There are no minimum spacing or leg room requirements for minibus seats, but there is a minimum permitted width of 400mm. No seats may be fitted to a door. Seats must be properly anchored to the minibus.

Electrical connections
If the electrical circuit is over 100 volts it must be protected by a dual pole switch accessible to the driver from inside the vehicle. This switch must not extinguish any of the vehicle's obligatory lamps.

Fuel tanks and exhaust pipes
No fuel tank must be located within the passenger compartment. Exhaust pipe outlets can only be at the rear or side of the minibus.

Step lights
All steps at passenger exits and gangways must be properly illuminated.

General
All bodywork and fittings must be soundly constructed and maintained in good serviceable condition. Drivers should therefore check periodically not only that their vehicles meet the above minimum requirements but also that seats are clean and not torn, there are no sharp or dangerous projections in the vehicle, windows are clean and floor coverings are not dangerously worn and that a fire extinguisher and first aid equipment are carried and readily available for use.

The carriage of highly flammable and dangerous substances in a minibus is prohibited unless these are so packed that no damage to the vehicle or injury to passengers is likely to result from an accident.

DRIVERS' HOURS AND RECORD KEEPING

The working hours of drivers are strictly controlled by legislation and European Community (EC) law prevails for the majority of commercial operations. Where vehicles, or the type of work being carried out, are exempt from EC law, British regulations, in the form of the Transport Act 1968 as modified, apply. If journeys are made to countries outside the European Community either the domestic laws of the country concerned must be adhered to, or if the country is a party to the European agreement on international road transport (AETR) those rules must be followed although in the latter case they have now been aligned with the EC Regulation 3820/85.

The regulations can be briefly summarised as follows.

1. EC Regulation 3820/85 applies to drivers operating passenger vehicles engaged on *Community regulated journeys or work* within the United Kingdom (known as national journeys) or to or from other Member States of the European Community (known as international journeys), ie Belgium, Denmark, Eire, France, Germany, Greece, Italy, Luxembourg, the Netherlands, Portugal and Spain.
2. AETR rules (which are now aligned with EC rules) apply to drivers operating passenger vehicles with nine or more passenger seats to countries which are outside the EC but are a party to the AETR agreement, ie Austria, the Czech Republic, Norway, the Slovak Republic, Sweden, USSR and the former Yugoslavia.
3. British domestic legislation applies to drivers who drive certain vehicles or perform certain types of work exempt from the EC rules. Some exemptions apply generally whilst others apply only to journeys within Great Britain. Passenger vehicles with 12 or fewer seats (excluding the driver's seat) are exempt from this legislation if the vehicle is not used for hire or reward operations ie private use.
4. Mixed driving is where a driver changes from driving under EC rules to driving under British rules and vice-versa.

In the following pages each set of rules is given in detail.

Drivers of vehicles used by the armed forces, police and fire brigades are exempt from the regulations.

A driver is anyone who drives a vehicle, either regularly or occasionally, or is carried on the vehicle in order to be available for driving if necessary; part time drivers such as maintenance staff and technicians or employees who have to use a vehicle as a means of transporting themselves in the course of the owner's business.

OFFENCES

It is an offence to contravene any part of the drivers' hours regulations and heavy fines can be imposed on a driver (up to £2500) if convicted. The employer may also be prosecuted and in very severe cases the employer can face a prison sentence — in these circumstances the operator's licence may also be put at risk.

It is, therefore, very important for a driver to fully understand the rules governing his working hours so that infringements are avoided.

Prohibition of certain types of payment
Under EC law it is an offence for payments in the form of bonuses, etc to be made for distance travelled if this is likely to endanger road safety.

"COMMUNITY REGULATED" JOURNEYS

EC Regulation 3820/85 applies to drivers of passenger vehicles with seats for 17 or more passengers (excluding the driver's seat) operating within the United Kingdom (known as national journeys) or with seats for nine or more passengers (excluding the driver's seat) operating to or from another Member State of the European Community (known as an international journeys) unless the vehicle or the operation is exempt. A list of the exemptions is given on page 82 but the most useful exemption applies to passenger vehicles on regular services, where the route covered by the service does not exceed 50km. A return journey over the same route is not included when determining route length. Therefore, Community regulations apply to a vehicle if it has nine or more passenger seats (17 or more on national journeys and work), and it is used on either:

(a) a regular service over 50km. This could include some regular contracts such as schools and works journeys,

if over this distance and longer distance regular services whether "express" or "stopping", or
(b) "occasional" and "shuttle" services. In practice these EC terms cover private hire work and excursions and tours — unless the latter have been registered as local services because they operate one or more times per week over at least six consecutive weeks.

In conjunction with the above-mentioned regulation, EC Regulation 3821/85 also applies and this is concerned with the type of record of their working hours that drivers must keep, namely the tachograph chart. Details of these regulations will be found on page 90.

Daily driving period

This is a maximum of *nine hours* which may be extended to *10 hours* maximum not more than twice a week.

The daily driving period is defined as being the period between any two daily rest periods or between a daily and a weekly rest period.

Weekly driving

Weekly driving is governed by the requirement that a driver must, after no more than six consecutive daily driving periods, take a weekly rest period.

Drivers on non-regular services may take a weekly rest, (equivalent to an aggregated first and second weeks' rests) after the end of 12 consecutive days' driving. This concession applies throughout the year.

Driving periods

In the case of *Kelly v Schulman (1988)* it was held that a driver may, after 6 driving periods (separated by daily rest periods) provided he has not exceeded the maximum permitted weekly driving hours, postpone his weekly rest period until the end of the sixth **day**. He may continue to drive during this period of postponement up to his maximum permitted weekly driving hours.

Total fortnightly driving

Total fortnightly driving is *90 hours* maximum.

Note: a driver can drive up to a total of *56 hours* in one week but is restricted to *34 hours* in the second so that over the two consecutive weeks the limit is not exceeded.

Driving time
A driver may drive for a total of 4½ hours (which can be either continuous or accumulated) after which a break must be taken.

Breaks from driving
After not more than a total of 4½ hours' driving a break of at least *45 minutes* must be taken unless the driver begins a rest period. This break can be split into shorter breaks which must be of at least 15 minutes duration so that they aggregate 45 minutes spread over the driving period or immediately following it. However, drivers should be careful not to follow a 4½ hour driving period split in this way with an uninterrupted second period of 4½ hours' driving since it could then be held that they would not have had a break of at least 45 minutes after totalling 4½ hours' aggregate driving.

During a break the driver must not carry out any other work. However, waiting time and time spent in the passenger seat of a vehicle in motion, on a ferry or a train, will not be regarded as other work.

Drivers on national journeys and work driving on regular services which have to call at certain London and large city termini may reduce the driving period of 4½ hours to four hours followed by a 30 minute break if it is not possible for them to comply with the above regulations.

The local authority areas to which this concession extends are (in London) the City of Westminster, the Royal Borough of Kensington and Chelsea and the Boroughs of Camden and Islington. Outside London the concession applies to:
  (a) Digbeth Coach Station, Birmingham and its vicinity
  (b) Marlborough Street Coach Station, Bristol and its vicinity
  (c) Wellington Street Coach Station, Leeds and its vicinity
  (d) St Margaret's Bus Station, Leicester and its vicinity
  (e) Victoria Bus Station, Nottingham and its vicinity
  (f) Oxpens Coach Park, Oxford and its vicinity.

Daily rest period
In each 24 hour period a driver must have a daily rest of at least *11 consecutive hours* which may be reduced to not less than *nine consecutive hours* on three days a week. Any reduction in the daily rest must be made up before the end of the *following week*. However, on days when the daily rest

period is not reduced a driver is allowed to split this 11 hours into two or three separate periods (minimum one hour) during the 24 hours, one period of which must be of at least *eight consecutive hours*. When the daily rest is split in this manner the minimum length of the daily rest must be increased to *12 hours*.

Where a vehicle is *double manned* each driver must have a rest period of not less than *eight consecutive hours* during each period of 30 hours (making the maximum permitted length of their working day 22 hours).

Daily rest periods may be taken in the vehicle provided it is fitted with a bunk and the vehicle is *stationary*.

In order to benefit from the Community drivers' hours relaxation for double manning the relief driver must travel in the vehicle at all times and not be shared between a number of vehicles in convoy.

Note: where journeys involve the use of ferries or trains, drivers may interrupt their daily rest period, not more than once, provided they comply with the following conditions:

(a) part of the daily rest period spent on land may be taken before or after that part of the daily rest period taken on board the ferry or train
(b) the period between the two parts must be as short as possible and must not exceed one hour before embarkation or after disembarkation
(c) drivers must have access to a bunk or couchette during both parts of the rest period
(d) where the daily rest period is interrupted in this way it must be increased by two hours
(e) when time spent on board a ferry or train is not counted as part of the daily rest period it will, instead, be regarded as a break — see under *Breaks from driving*.

Weekly rest period

During each week a daily rest period must be extended into a weekly rest period totalling *45 consecutive hours*, however this may be reduced to *36 consecutive hours* if taken where the vehicle or driver is normally based, or to a minimum of *24 consecutive hours* if taken elsewhere. Each reduced rest period must be made good by the driver taking an equivalent rest period *en bloc* before the end of the *third week* following the week in question.

A weekly rest period beginning in one week and continuing into the next can be attached to either week.

Any compensatory rest period taken for the reduced daily and/or weekly rest periods must be attached to another rest period of at least *eight hours* and be granted at the request of the driver at the vehicle's parking place or driver's base.

The definition of a week is the period between 00.00 hours Monday and 24.00 hours Sunday.

Emergencies

Article 12 of the regulations allows a driver, provided that road safety is not jeopardised, to depart from the driving restrictions to enable him to reach a suitable stopping place to ensure the safety of persons and of the vehicle. In these circumstances the reason must be recorded on the tachograph chart. (For details of the tachograph regulations see page 94.)

Periodic checks

Article 15 requires an employer to organise work in such a way that drivers do not infringe either the hours or the tachograph rules. It further requires employers to make periodic checks to ensure that the regulations have been complied with. If breaches are found steps must be taken to prevent their repetition.

Exemptions

The following are exempt from EC regulations.

1. Vehicles used for the carriage of passengers constructed or equipped to carry not more than nine persons including the driver (but see item 7 below).
2. Vehicles used by or under the control of the armed services, civil defence, fire services, and forces responsible for maintaining public order.
3. Vehicles used in emergency or rescue operations.
4. Specialised vehicles used for medical purposes (ambulances).
5. Specialised breakdown vehicles.
6. Vehicles undergoing road tests for technical development, repair or maintenance purposes, and new or rebuilt vehicles which are not yet in service.

In addition to the above the following are exempt when *operating within the United Kingdom.*

7. Vehicles used for the carriage of passengers and constructed or equipped to carry not more than 17 persons including the driver and intended for that purpose.
8. Vehicles which, on or after *1.1.90,* are being used by a public authority to provide public services. **Note:** vehicles falling within this description are vehicles:
   (a) being used by a health authority in England and Wales or a Health Board in Scotland or the Common Services Agency for the Scottish Health Service
   (b) providing an ambulance service under the National Health Service Act 1977 or the National Health Service (Scotland) Act 1978; or carrying staff, patients, medical supplies or equipment as part of its general duties under those Acts
   (c) being used by a local authority under the Local Authority Social Service Act 1970 or the Social Work (Scotland) Act 1968 to provide certain social services
   (d) being used by HM Coastguard; a general or local lighthouse authority; a harbour authority; airports authority within the perimeter of an airport
   (e) being used by the British Railways Board, London Regional Transport or any wholly owned subsidiary of LRT, a Passenger Transport Executive or a local authority for railway maintenance
   (f) being used by the British Waterways Board for navigable waterway maintenance.
9. Vehicles operating exclusively on an island not exceeding 2300km^2 in area and which is not connected to the rest of Great Britain by a bridge, ford or tunnel. **Note:** this includes the Isle of Wight, Arran and Bute.
10. A vehicle being used for driving instruction with a view to obtaining a driving licence.

Summary of EC Drivers' Hours Regulations for PSVs

	MAX/MIN	BASIC RULE	RELAXATION
On driving without a break	Max	4h 30mins	Regular services calling at certain London and large city termini 4h
On breaks	Min	45mins	Up to 3 breaks of at least 15mins

	MAX/MIN	BASIC RULE	RELAXATION
On driving time	Max	9h	2×10 hours in fixed week
On length of working day	Max	24−11=13h*	24−9=15h*
On length of working day if double manned	Max	22h	
On rest	Min	11h	3×9h in fixed week compensated by end of following week
Split rest		12h total =	1 rest 8h minimum + up to 2 more 1h minimum to total 12h
On rest if double manned	Min	8h/30h	—
On driving time	Max	6×9=54h	(2×10)+(4×9)=56h
On fortnightly driving time	Max	90h	—
On rest	Min	45h after 6 consecutive days' driving (12 days for non-regular drivers but followed by at least 1 weekly rest)	36h working from base 24h working away from base. Compensate 'en block' within 3 weeks

KEY

1. Fixed week commences Sunday at midnight.
2. * can be inferred from other limits.

AETR

The European Agreement concerning the work of crews of vehicles engaged in international road transport, AETR, is not an EC agreement but embodies a larger group of European countries which includes the United Kingdom and other EC Member States.

Countries outside the EC which are parties to the agreement include Austria, the Czech Republic, Norway, the Slovak Republic, Sweden, USSR and the former Yugoslavia. When drivers are travelling to these countries they should comply with the same regulations as for EC related journeys (see page 78).

BRITISH DOMESTIC OPERATIONS

Domestic legislation in the form of the Transport Act 1968 Part VI, as modified, applies within Great Britain to drivers of vehicles which are exempt from EC law.

Operations covered

Operations which come within the jurisdiction of British hours law are listed below (unless they are covered by some other exemption).

1. Vehicles used for the carriage of passengers constructed or equipped to carry not more than 17 persons including the driver.
2. Vehicles on regular services where the route does not exceed 50 km, including local services, excursions and tours registered as such, and regular contracts such as schools and works services.
3. Vehicles used in emergency or rescue operations.
4. Specialised vehicles used for medical purposes including ambulances.
5. Specialised breakdown vehicles.
6. Vehicles undergoing road tests for technical development, repair or maintenance purposes and new or rebuilt vehicles which are not yet in service.
7. Vehicles operating exclusively on an island not exceeding 2300km^2 in area and which is not connected to the rest of Great Britain by a bridge, ford or tunnel.
8. A vehicle propelled by gas produced on the vehicle or a vehicle propelled by electricity, having a permissible maximum weight not exceeding 7.5 tonnes.
9. A vehicle being used for driving instruction with a view to obtaining a driving licence.

Domestic hours limits

The provisions of the Transport Act 1968 apply. However these were relaxed in 1971 by the Drivers' Hours (Passenger and Goods Vehicles) (Modifications) Order 1971 to exclude any limits on the amounts of daily and weekly duty apart from a prescribed maximum length of working day.

Maximum total daily driving time

No driver may drive a vehicle for an aggregate time in excess of 10 hours per working day.

Continuous driving without a break

A driver must take a break of at least *30 minutes* after driving continuously (ie without the driving being broken by breaks satisfying the minimum length requirements) for 5½ *hours*. Any other interruptions from driving (not including any shorter breaks which are intended to be aggregated to 45 minutes as below) for non-driving work can be completely ignored for the purposes of calculating the continuous driving limits, based on the cumulative aggregate of actual periods of driving.

The Drivers' Hours (Passenger and Goods Vehicles) (Modifications) Order 1971 (SI 1971 No. 818) provides an important alternative to the 5½ hours' duty rule based on continuous driving. Under these rules a driver may drive for up to 8½ hours straight through provided that he or she takes breaks of non-driving time, eg layover at terminals, etc amounting in aggregate to at least 45 minutes and that the last of the driving periods marks either the end of the working day or the start of a 30 minute break.

Thus, this provision means that the 8½ hour "duty" need not be the only work on that day.

Maximum daily duty/spreadover

The maximum daily duty (working day) for drivers performing domestic journeys and work is precisely prescribed by the Drivers' Hours (Passenger and Goods Vehicles) (Modifications) Order 1971 (SI 1971 No. 818) which provides for a maximum spreadover each working day of *16 hours*, which, apart from statutory break periods, may include up to *10 hours'* driving and the remainder as work other than driving.

Daily intervals of rest

A driver must have a period of rest under the 1971 Modifications Order of at least *10 hours* between each working day. This can be reduced on three days in the working week to 8½ hours.

Note: a working day is not a calendar day. It is a period of driving and duty separated by two statutory periods for rest. (It is of course impossible to legislate for a period of rest since the driver is free to take rest or otherwise.)

Minimum weekly rest

The Transport Act 1968 provides that a driver must have a period of at least *24 hours* off duty in a working week. However, the 1971 Modifications Order, provides for a rest day of *24 hours every two weeks*, ie each fortnight. The rest period does not have to be a calendar day. It can be taken at the beginning or end of a working fortnight and can fall partly in one fortnight and partly in the next, provided it is started in the fortnight to which it applies.

The strict interpretation (for drivers working under domestic rules) of 24 hours in every two consecutive weeks means that it is possible to satisfy the requirement by having off day 1 of week 1, with the next rest commencing sometime during day 7 of week 3 (ie the 20th day).

Driving time

Driving is time spent at the controls of the vehicle for the purpose of controlling its movement whether it is in motion or not. If some driving is done off the road, eg within the private grounds of an educational establishment, this does not count as driving time but as part of the duty time.

Light vans and dual-purpose vehicles

Drivers of light vans (not exceeding 3.5 tonnes permissible maximum weight) and dual-purpose vehicles are subject only to the 10 hour driving regulations when engaged solely in certain professional activities, ie doctors, dentists, nurses, midwives, veterinary surgeons, commercial travellers, employees of the AA, RAC and RSAC and persons using their vehicles to assist in carrying out any service of inspection, cleaning, maintenance, repair, installation or fitting. Also included are cinematography, radio or television broadcasting staff.

Emergencies

Where events cause, or are likely to cause danger to life or health of persons or animals, serious interruption in the maintenance of public services for the supply of water, gas, electricity or drainage or of telecommunication or postal services, or a serious interruption in the use of roads, railways, ports or airports, driving and duty limits may be exceeded provided the driver does not spend time on duty (other than to deal with the emergency) for periods aggregating more than 11 hours.

PSV Drivers' Hours - Domestic

	MAX/MIN	BASIC RULE	RELAXATION
On driving without a break	Max	5h 30mins	8h 30mins with 45min aggregate breaks
On breaks	Min	30mins	45min aggregate break in 8h 30mins and followed by 30mins if this not end of working day
On driving time	Max	10h	—
On length of working day	Max	16h	—
On rest	Min	10h	3 × 8h 30mins in fixed week
On rest	Min	24h each 2 fixed weeks	—

MIXED DRIVING

This concerns drivers who change from community regulated operations to British domestic operations. In instances where this occurs the driver has the choice of observing the EC rules all the time, or a combination of both provided the EC limits are not exceeded when engaged on EC work. The following points must also be considered.
1. Time spent driving under EC rules does not count as "off duty" under domestic rules.
2. Time spent operating under domestic rules does not count as a break or rest under Community rules.
3. Driving time under EC rules counts towards the driving and duty limits under domestic rules.
4. If any EC driving is undertaken in a week the driver must observe the EC daily and weekly rest requirements.

What counts as duty?

Although the only specific limits on duty time occur in the domestic regulations, where the maximum length of the working day (or spreadover) is 16 hours, it is nevertheless important to be able to determine what constitutes being on duty since this may, under both domestic and Community regulations, impinge on daily or weekly rest time.

Duty time

Obviously time spent on duty by an employee driving a passenger vehicle will count as duty, as will driving by an owner-driver in connection with his business. In addition it should be appreciated that under Community regulations any time spent driving a passenger vehicle within the scope of the regulations (whether or not as part of a driver's employment) counts as driving time and hence also duty.

However, duty also includes any other time spent acting under an employer's specific instructions. An employee will generally not be considered to be on duty during breaks for rest and refreshment if during those breaks he or she has no specific duties or responsibilities to discharge for the employer.

United Kingdom case law has established that duty embraces any activity from which an employer (or self-employed owner-driver) gains a benefit, or where the driver is under the control of the employer. Note that the fact that payment has been made is not conclusive evidence that a driver was on duty — the payment may, for example, be a bonus or overtime.

The DOT has issued guidelines as to what constitutes, or does not constitute, duty for the purpose of implementing the domestic hours regulations.

A driver is considered to be on duty when:
(a) travelling to take over a bus after "signing on"
(b) awaiting allocation of work on the "spare" rota. (The driver will, however, be "off duty" if released early before the end of his or her rostered spell on the "spare", even if paid to the end of that time. This could bring forward the driver's earliest available time for work the following day)
(c) working for a second employer as a driver
(d) double manning
(e) conducting
(f) in charge of the vehicle during "layover" time at a terminus
(g) inspecting or collecting data
(h) working for a second employer for whom no driving is done. (**NB** this applies only on Community journeys and work — see below.)

A driver is off duty:
(a) when taking a rostered meal break

(b) during the mid period of a "split" or "spreadover" duty (whether paid or unpaid)

(c) when waiting at a destination for a private hire party (eg as a spectator at a football match).

Two or more employers

Most of the above guidelines would apply equally to Community regulated journeys and work, but Community law counts non-driving work for another employer as impinging on rest limits.

Exemptions from British domestic hours regulations for part time drivers

Drivers on domestic journeys and work who do not drive for more than four hours per day in any one week do not have to observe any hours rules during that week.

On two working days per week they may drive over four hours and on each of these two days:

(a) all duties must start and finish within that 24 hour "day"

(b) driving time must not exceed 10 hours

(c) working time must not exceed 16 hours

(d) there must be 10 hours' rest preceding and following each working day

(e) if one of the days overlaps into a week in which the part time driving exemption does not apply, limits on driving and spreadover must be observed.

Note: The rule is applicable:
(a) week by week, not day by day
(b) to hours of work, not records of work.

DRIVERS' HOURS OF WORK RECORDS

The tachograph

Drivers who are subject to EC Regulation 3820/85 must also observe the requirements of EC Regulation 3821/85 (also applicable to AETR related journeys) which concerns the recording of a driver's working hours by means of the tachograph.

However, as an alternative to the tachograph, drivers of vehicles on national regular services may carry a timetable and duty roster (see below).

Since drivers on regular services not exceeding 50km route length are exempt from EC drivers' hours and the need to use a tachograph, this exemption is in effect only applied to drivers on regular services over 50km route length.

It is also available to drivers on regular international services which are cross-border services which start and finish not more than 50km "as the crow flies" from each border and where the route length, by road, does not exceed 100km.

The tachograph is an instrument (see illustration on page 92) which automatically records, by means of a chart positioned behind the clock face:

(a) the distance travelled by the vehicle
(b) the vehicle's speed
(c) the driving time
(d) the periods of work of the driver
(e) breaks in the working day and daily rest period and
(f) the opening of the case containing the record chart.

It is so constructed that the driver is able to observe that the instrument is recording properly; that the last nine hours on the chart are visible to an examiner without the need to take any action other than opening the tachograph; and that when a second driver is carried on the vehicle his or her attendance is recorded on a separate chart.

Note: If a second driver is carried on the vehicle the instrument must be capable of recording both drivers' hours of work, therefore a two person tachograph must be fitted and when the second driver begins driving the charts must be changed over to record this driving period.

On top of the instrument is the driver mode control selector with the symbols:

- ⊗ — Driving periods
- ▱ — Working periods
- ⊨ — Rest periods
- ⚒ — Other working periods — but this symbol is not used in Great Britain.

Two Driver Tachograph

Front View

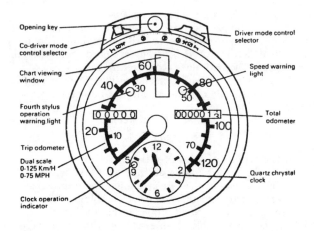

When performing any function covered by these symbols the mode selector must be set against the correct symbol otherwise the recording on the chart will be incorrect. This is an offence which could lead to prosecution.

As an example, if, during a working day averaging nine hours, the mode selector is set on the "wheel" and is not changed, the record will show no breaks having been taken, the chart will only record that during the day the vehicle was stationary for a certain period of time. Since it is a requirement of the law that a break of at least 45 minutes must be taken after a total of $4\frac{1}{2}$ hours' driving, there would be no indication from the recorded details that such a break had been observed and this would be an infringement of the drivers' hours rules, which would leave the driver open to prosecution.

It is, therefore, most important that the instrument is used correctly.

Instrument checks The instrument must be *checked* every two years and *recalibrated* every six. Plaques are attached to it showing the date when the inspections are carried out. The two yearly checks are due either two years after the date shown on the installation plaque or two years after the date shown on the two yearly plaque, whichever is the later.

The six yearly recalibration is due six years after the date shown on the *installation* plaque regardless of any two yearly inspections.

At the time of recalibration all existing plaques are removed and the next inspection is then due two years later.

In some cases the two and six yearly inspections may never be reached, because if the instrument develops a fault it must be examined and repaired at a tachograph centre. When this happens a new plaque is attached to it which means that the time limits start again.

The two yearly plaque is in this format:

```
TWO YEARLY INSPECTION
Centre/Seal No...................
Date............................
```

whilst the six yearly recalibration plaque is similar to this:

```
Date............................
'1'.........................mm
'w'.............................
rev/km
                         imp/km
Seal No .........................
```

Failure to comply with these requirements can incur a fine on summary conviction.

Example of a Used Tachograph Chart

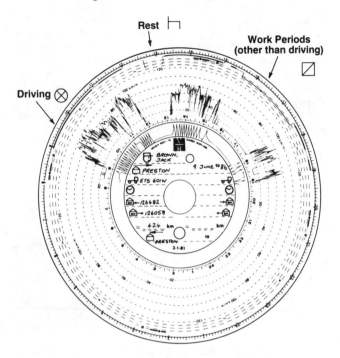

The chart The chart (see illustration above) is a specially wax-coated disc which comprises a centre field for recording certain particulars by hand. Radiating outwards are various concentric rings — the first being a distance (km) trace, followed by the various activity symbols and finally the speed symbol. On the outer edge are the time segments up to 24 hours.

Note: there are variations in the make-up of different types of charts, depending on the make of instrument used, but the basic information remains the same.

The distance, activity and speed traces are all marked automatically by the various styli and it is apparent from this that the mode selector referred to earlier must always be correctly positioned for the activity being carried out.

Care must be taken in handling charts as they can scratch and become damaged quite easily. By law damaged or dirty charts must not be used.

The chart must always face upwards when placed in the instrument.

Important: In some tachographs it is necessary to have a blind chart inserted when the vehicle is not in use to protect the styli from being damaged; this is because the mechanism continues to revolve whilst the clock is operating.

The instrument also has a speed warning light which allows a maximum operational speed to be set by the operator and if the limit is exceeded the warning light is illuminated. Drivers should be advised by their employers if operational speeds are set.

Drivers' responsibilities It is the driver's responsibility to complete the charts correctly and this means that from the moment of taking over the vehicle the driver must use a chart to record his or her driving and working time, etc. Before inserting the chart in the tachograph, the following particulars must be entered in the centre field:

(a) surname and first name
(b) the date and place of commencement of chart
(c) the registration number of the vehicle
(d) the odometer reading at the start of the first journey.

At the end of the working period the centre field must again be completed by recording:

(a) the final odometer reading
(b) the place of finishing
(c) the date.

If, during a working period, a change of vehicle takes place, this must be recorded on the chart (there is usually space on it to record at least two changes) and particulars of the new vehicle, together with the time of change, noted. If the second vehicle has a different make of tachograph, a chart compatible with the instrument must be used and the same procedure applied. At the end of the day all charts used must be kept together so that a complete record is available.

Whilst in charge of the vehicle the driver is responsible for seeing that the instrument is working correctly and that the mode is set properly for recording the various activities.

The time recorded on the chart must agree with the official time in the country of registration of the vehicle. (If it is an international journey the clock should be set at the official time in Great Britain and not changed on entering different time zones abroad.) The driver must also check that the time of day is correct when placing the chart in the instrument, ie if it is 7 am the chart should not start recording from 19.00 hours.

The driver must have in his or her possession the completed current week's charts and the chart for the last day of the previous week on which he or she drove for possible inspection by the enforcement authorities. Completed charts must be returned to the employer within 21 days. Failure to return charts within the time limit is an offence and carries a heavy fine on summary conviction.

A driver must be able to produce, to an authorised examiner at any time during the prescribed period, each chart used in the tachograph. The examiner can enter the vehicle and inspect the instrument and inspect and copy or, if he suspects them of being false or having been tampered with, remove any charts found therein. Although there is no laid down procedure it is recommended that if a chart is removed by an authorised examiner or police officer for checking, a receipt is obtained showing the data and time of the occurrence. If a new chart has to be fitted the official should be asked to note the circumstances on that chart.

If the tachograph develops a fault or ceases to function, manual records must continue to be made of the various activities, either on the chart, on a temporary chart or a sheet of paper. Whatever method is used the original chart plus any temporary chart or sheet of paper must be kept together so that a complete record of the working period is available. On returning to the depot the employer must be notified so that arrangements can be made for repairs to be carried out at an approved centre. It is a legal requirement that the instrument must be repaired as soon as circumstances permit. However, if the vehicle is unlikely to return to the depot within a period of one week calculated from the day of the breakdown or discovery of defective operation, the repair must be carried out en route.

When the tachograph was originally installed it will have been calibrated and sealed — there can be at least six seals attached to it — and these seals must not be tampered with.

If the seals are broken for any reason the circumstances must be noted and the employer informed so that new seals can be attached by a tachograph centre (see also *Instrument checks* above).

Repairs, recalibration and sealing can only take place at an approved tachograph centre; if for any reason there is a delay in having the instrument attended to, the driver should carry in the cab either a note or some other proof that the vehicle has been booked in for repair on a certain date. This should satisfy an examiner if the driver is stopped during a period when manual records are being kept because of the state of the instrument.

If a chart is damaged during a working day it must not be thrown away but kept and at the end of the working period attached to the replacement chart in the tachograph.

Two or more employers If a driver works for more than one employer each employer must be notified of the name and address of the other(s) and completed charts must be returned to the first employer irrespective of who supplied the charts.

Failure to notify each employer of the circumstances is an offence and can incur a heavy fine on summary conviction.

A driver has the right to ask the employer for copies of completed charts.

Employers' responsibilities It is the employer's responsibility to issue sufficient charts for the operation involved, bearing in mind the possibility of charts being damaged or removed by law enforcement officers. It is therefore a good idea for the driver to have at least seven days' supply.

The charts must be suitable for the instrument fitted in the vehicle being used. They are not interchangeable between different makes of instrument.

The employer must ensure that completed charts are returned within 21 days and the charts must be kept in good order for at least 12 months and be made available for inspection by law enforcement officers if required.

All these requirements apply equally to the owner-driver. Employers must give copies of record sheets to employees who ask for them.

Records used in evidence The record produced by the tachograph and any manual entries made on the chart may be evidence, and in Scotland sufficient evidence, of the matters appearing from them as they affect drivers' hours and record keeping. Other records which also show on the chart, eg a vehicle exceeding the speed limit, will not normally be accepted as evidence unless it is corroborated by other evidence such as a police patrol or radar check.

Offences Apart from the offences already mentioned, it is an offence:
 (a) if the vehicle to which the regulations apply does not have a tachograph or
 (b) if the instrument is installed and is not being used in accordance with the regulations, eg tampering with the instrument to produce false records, etc.

Fines of up to £5000 can be imposed on summary conviction.

It is a defence when it is proved that:
 (a) the vehicle was proceeding to a tachograph centre for the equipment to be installed
 (b) the equipment was not working correctly because it could not be repaired by an approved fitter or workshop
 (c) manual recordings were being made by drivers whilst the equipment was inoperable.

Similarly, where seals are broken or removed, it is not an offence if:
 (a) the action was unavoidable
 (b) it was not possible for the seals to be replaced by an approved fitter or workshop
 (c) the equipment in all other respects was being used in accordance with the regulations.

Reminders The centre field of the chart must be completed *before* replacing it in the instrument and again when finishing the working day or when a change of vehicle takes place.

If working away from the vehicle for any length of time the driver should make sure that the mode selector is correctly positioned for recording the working time; alternatively, the chart should be removed and details entered by hand (this is especially important if the vehicle is left standing for any period, ie in the yard where someone else could drive it). The driver may also be taking a statutory break during this period, which must be recorded.

Drivers should remember to operate the mode selector switch so that it is recording the work actually being performed at any given time (see page 92).

The EC regulations provide that where the driver is away from the vehicle and unable to operate the equipment in person, the various records of time must (either manually or by automatic recording or otherwise) be legibly entered on the sheet without damaging it. *Thus there is no legal requirement to leave charts in tachographs overnight but if operating on a journey outside the United Kingdom it is advisable to leave the chart in the instrument until replaced by a new chart (but not longer than 24 hours). Enforcement authorities in some other EC countries will not accept manual entries on the chart face other than those required in the centre field.*

The chart can be left in the instrument for up to 24 hours but it is advisable only to do this if it is certain that the vehicle will not be moved during the driver's absence and that the driver will return before the chart overruns.

Drivers should note that the chart is a personal record of the hours they have worked; it is not a log for the vehicle.

Service timetable and duty roster

Drivers on regular services within the United Kingdom may, as an alternative to using a tachograph, carry with them a timetable and duty roster. A regular service is a service operating at specified intervals along specified routes calling at predetermined stops.

Operators must construct a service timetable and duty roster and a copy of that part relating to the driver's own route must be carried on the vehicle.

The service timetable must show the pattern of the service in sufficient detail to indicate that it is being followed and the driver must carry a copy whilst at work.

The duty roster must show each driver's name, date of birth, base and duty schedule for the current week, the preceding week and the following week (three weeks in all). The schedule must show the driver's daily rest periods, breaks, driving periods, and other periods of duty. It must be signed by the service operator and the driver must carry his or her own personal extract whilst at work. It must be kept by the operator for one year after the expiry of the period covered. Drivers must be given extracts from it if they so request.

Exemptions A driver does not have to keep records if driving a passenger vehicle with 17 or fewer seats (nine on journeys outside the United Kingdom) including the driver's seat or a passenger vehicle on a "regular service" under 50km in route length.

Note: Whilst record keeping is not required in these circumstances, an employer has the right to ask the driver to keep some form of record to comply with company requirements.

RESPONSIBILITIES OF THE DRIVER

CUSTOMER CARE — UNDERSTANDING AND HELPING PASSENGERS

Before bus de-regulation operators of local services held road service licences which usually gave them a monopoly on their route. Passengers had no alternative choice of service, although they could, of course, sometimes choose to walk, cycle or take their cars.

Coach operators performing private hires (and, since 1980, express services and excursions and tours of over 30 miles) have always had to compete for passengers and their staff have generally understood the importance of maintaining the good customer relations upon which their jobs depended.

Passenger relations

A driver's relationship with the passengers will be good, and their custom will be retained, if he or she provides the *service* which they want (and for which they are paying). Service and servility should not be confused — it is not necessary to be servile to create a good image of the service and keep the passengers happy.

The driver's image

Drivers should remember that they are often the first point of contact between the passenger and the company. The odd passenger may have formed an initial impression of the service from the way he has been dealt with when making a telephone enquiry or from speaking to an inspector, and certainly other employees have an important customer care role too, but the drivers' role is paramount. Drivers can reinforce the first good impression or repair an initial poor impression.

Bus drivers are exposed to the public like actors on stage. Their behaviour reflects on the undertaking. Even when drivers are relaxing and talking amongst themselves, they must be careful not to be critical of their supervisors or mates within earshot of passengers!

Passengers observe the cleanliness of the vehicle, the way in which it is driven and the driver's timekeeping. A smooth ride is not only the mark of a professional driver, it is also excellent for customer relations.

When passengers board a vehicle it is not usually with the express purpose of having a nice ride — it is because they want to arrive at a destination in safety and on time. The nice ride is a bonus.

The price of arriving safely and on time is the fare, which the driver must charge the passenger. Psychologists have found that although passengers do not perceive the payment of a fare as distressing, it is precisely that — a "distress purchase" in marketing jargon. In other words it does not give the same immediate pleasure as, for example, the purchase of an ice cream or a pint of beer but it relieves them of the cash which they would rather have spent on beer or ice cream!

Interestingly, passengers don't perceive off the bus sales in the same light, which is one good reason for operators promoting these — they are good for passenger relations!

Not surprisingly, then, many driver/passenger confrontations arise at the farebox, (or when fare payment is being checked by an inspector).

Understanding passengers To avoid needless confrontations drivers need to be able to understand their passengers. Many passengers are insecure but try to hide their insecurity because no one likes to look foolish in public. The insecurity can arise in many ways:

(a) they may not know the fare to their destination and are afraid to ask the driver because he or she looks unfriendly

(b) they may be afraid of being late for an appointment or a connection

(c) they may be afraid of boarding the wrong vehicle and going astray

(d) they may be having difficulty disentangling complex information on signs, bus stop display boards or timetables (services are changing so rapidly after de-regulation that it is easy to sympathise with confused passengers — many drivers are equally confused)

(e) they may have children or elderly persons "in tow"

(f) they may be young, elderly or disabled themselves

(g) bus stations, airports and railway terminals are confusing places, scenes of hectic activity, and passengers can easily become confused and insecure.

Good passenger care simply involves recognising passenger anxiety, making allowances for irrational passenger behaviour and trying to be helpful and reassuring.

Product knowledge Drivers must know their product, ie they must know the fare tables, different types of passes and tokens, timetables and connecting services. They should be prepared to be asked questions and to answer them effectively.

Communication It is the driver's job to communicate with passengers. Whether this is done on an individual basis or collectively (perhaps using a public address system), the rules are the same:

(a) be prepared — drivers must know what they want to say ("Engage mind before opening mouth" is excellent advice which all drivers should understand!)

(b) be calm — driving is a stressful job, even if the passenger is ruffled, this must not affect the driver - it will do no good

(c) be assertive — drivers should not be bossy, just positive, so that there is no misunderstanding about what they are saying. If the fare is more than a passenger thinks it is, for example, the driver should show him the fare table, there is no need to apologise!

(d) be concerned — most drivers show concern when a blind passenger boards their bus, yet many drivers fail to recognise the disability of travel anxiety

(e) be pleasant — a smile is free but can do more to win passengers than all the advice given so far! One large operator even tells enquiry staff to "smile on the phone". Oddly enough, even though the people at the other end cannot see the smile, they can often pick up the warmth in the voice which accompanies a smile.

When things go wrong There is little point pretending everything is fine when the passengers can see for themselves that it isn't! If drivers explain difficulties and delays passengers will usually accept the situation and may even be supportive. Drivers should keep passengers informed about what is being done to correct the problem. Passengers do not like being kept in the dark and can very quickly revert to a state of acute travel anxiety.

Dealing with complaints Because drivers are the initial, and sometimes only, point of contact between passengers and the operator, they will receive their share of complaints. Some of these will be justified, others will be genuine but arise out of a misunderstanding or misinformation. A few will be unjustified.

Most, but not all, people find it difficult to complain. If a passenger feels that he has a genuine complaint, he wants to be reassured that it will be taken seriously. So drivers should always acknowledge complaints. Obviously, if they can deal with it they should do so but if not, they should offer to pass it on to the person who can deal with it, or give the passenger details of how he can make the complaint formally if he does not wish the driver to do so.

Most passengers will be happy for drivers to take up their complaints for them if they feel that the drivers can be trusted to do so. Of course it goes without saying that the complaint must then be passed on, so it is a good idea to get a name and address or telephone number so that passengers can be informed of the outcome of their complaints.

Summary Drivers are the ambassadors of the company for which they drive. They are in full view of passengers whom they have to keep happy, secure and informed. To a large extent, drivers create their company's image.

CONDUCT OF DRIVERS, PASSENGERS, ETC

Apart from the requirement by employers for their drivers to behave in a proper manner at all times when on duty, the PSV (Conduct of Drivers, Inspectors, Conductors and Passengers) Regulations 1990 (SI 1020) contain provisions which they are bound to observe.

Drivers must stop their bus as closely as possible to the left or nearside when picking up or setting down passengers, and take reasonable precautions for the safety of boarding, travelling or alighting passengers (the latter provisions must also be observed by any *conductor* carried on the vehicle).

Conductors and passengers must not distract the driver's attention or obscure his vision whilst the vehicle is moving without having reasonable cause.

Drivers, inspectors or conductors must take all reasonable steps to ensure that passengers comply with the regulations. They must give particulars of their employer's name and address to any police constable or person having reasonable grounds for requiring it, and, in the case of the driver, details of his licence.

Smoking

Drivers, inspectors and conductors must not smoke on a vehicle except:
  (a) in a part of the vehicle where smoking is *not* prohibited so long as the vehicle is not available for carrying passengers
  (b) where the vehicle is hired as a whole (eg private hire) and permission to smoke has been granted by the *operator* and the *hirer*.

Passengers must not smoke or carry lit tobacco in any part of a vehicle designated a non-smoking area by notice, except where the vehicle is hired as a whole and the prohibition has been waived by *both operator* and *hirer*.

Microphones

Drivers may not use a microphone or communicate with anyone directly whilst the vehicle is moving except:
  (a) where it is essential to do so in an emergency or to deal with safety matters
  (b) to communicate with a "relevant person" (the operator or an employee of the operator) on an operational matter so long as he can do so without being distracted from driving the vehicle. *This provision permits the use of bus radios*
  (c) to indicate by means of occasional short statements the location of a vehicle when operating a service for hire and reward at separate fares (except an excursion and tour or sightseeing service) so long as he can do so without being distracted from driving the vehicle.

Passengers on PSVs must also not:
(a) unless directed by a driver, inspector or conductor, use any entrance or exit other than for the purpose which is indicated
(b) impede any boarding or alighting passengers
(c) endanger the safety of, or cause discomfort to, other passengers
(d) trail or throw anything from the vehicle
(e) distribute any printed matter which either seeks or gives information or seeks comment, or offer anything for sale, without the operator's permission
(f) give any signal which might be interpreted by the driver as a signal to start the bus or to stop the bus in an emergency
(g) travel in a part of the vehicle not available for carrying passengers
(h) use or play any noisy musical instrument (including a radio, tape recorder, etc) which may annoy other passengers
(i) refuse to leave the vehicle when instructed by the driver, conductor or inspector because either:
   (i) the vehicle is full *or*
   (ii) the passenger has caused a nuisance *or*
   (iii) the passenger's condition is offensive to other passengers
   (iv) the passenger's clothing is in such a condition that it might soil the clothing of others or the fittings of the vehicle.
(j) deliberately interfere with the vehicle's fitted equipment.

Animals
Passengers with accompanying animals must comply with the instructions of the driver, conductor or inspector. If requested they must remove the animal from the bus.

Such a request must not be made of a blind person in respect of his guide dog unless the vehicle is a double decker or a single decker over 8.5m in length and there are already two or more dogs on board, or, in any other case, there is already one or more dogs on board.

Bulky, dangerous or cumbersome articles
Passengers with such articles must comply with the instructions of the driver, conductor or inspector as regards where on the

vehicle these are to be stowed. If requested they must remove the article from the bus.

Such articles will include those which:
(a) are bulky or cumbersome
(b) might be annoying to anyone on the vehicle
(c) might cause injury or danger to anyone on the vehicle
(d) might damage the vehicle or the property of a passenger.

Payment of fares

A fare is defined in the regulations as an amount paid by a passenger which can be calculated by him from a fare table carried on the vehicle.

If requested, a passenger must state the journey he intends to take or is taking, and must pay the full fare for the journey.

Payment must be made either to the driver when boarding a one person operated bus, or on request to the conductor, or the passenger must use appropriate fare collection or ticket cancelling equipment.

The passenger must leave the vehicle when the journey for which the fare has been paid is completed, or pay the fare for any further journey. *The regulations, in specifying the fare (***not excess*** fare) for any further journey, effectively create the offence of overriding.*

It should be noted that some operators have obtained statutory powers which enable them to charge a penalty fare in the event of a passenger failing to pay the correct, or any, fare.

Other operators attempt to achieve the same ends by including in all their fare tables a hefty "standard fare" (in effect a penalty fare) payable in the event of the correct fare for the journey not being paid.

Tickets

Passengers must not use tickets which are defaced, have been altered, issued to someone else and are not transferable, or which are expired. Any such ticket, or one issued in error, must be surrendered to the driver, conductor or inspector if so requested.

Any ticket issued for the journey (including pre-purchased tickets) must be retained by the passenger for the duration of his journey and be made available for inspection by the driver, inspector or conductor.

Removal of passengers from the bus

The driver, inspector or conductor may request the name and address of any passenger who they suspect of contravening the regulations and may remove from the bus any passenger who has contravened these regulations or may seek the assistance of a police constable who is then empowered to remove the passenger.

If the passenger refuses to give his name and address to the constable or satisfactorily to answer questions put to him for the purpose of checking his name and address, the constable may arrest him without warrant (Public Passenger Vehicles Act 1981 s.25(2)).

Non compliance with the regulations is an offence for which the maximum fine is £500.

The obligation to carry passengers

Operators have a legal obligation to carry all passengers who present themselves for carriage at the proper place and time. A driver is not at liberty to refuse, without good reason, to carry any passenger who is in a fit condition and is prepared to pay the fare and for whom there is room on his vehicle. A driver may, however, refuse a drunken, riotous or offensive person likey to cause annoyance or injury to other passengers and indeed would be in breach of his or her duty of care to the passengers were he or she not to do so.

A PSV operator normally has standard terms and conditions of carriage but if these are so restrictive as to attempt to remove the operator's absolute liability for the safety of the passengers, the Public Passenger Vehicles Act 1981 provides that they will be unenforceable.

Operators are liable to those passengers with whom they make a contract of carriage for their own negligence and for that of their servants. The contract is made by the passengers boarding the vehicle, since this action is taken to signify their willingness to pay the fare.

In most cases the existence of a contract of carriage is obvious because the passenger buys a ticket and there is usually a statement such as "Carried subject to terms and conditions of XYZ Bus Co" printed on the ticket.

Of course, some passengers are carried "gratuitously", ie they pay no fare. However, the Courts have held that such gratuitous passengers as pensioners or employees with free passes none the less have a "licence" to be on the vehicle and that the operator's liability under the laws of negligence cannot be any more restrictive than it can under a contract of carriage. (Drivers can be reassured that as employees they are further protected by their employers' compulsory employee liability insurance.)

An operator is liable for the safety of passengers' luggage carried on a PSV, unless the passenger takes charge of it. The driver's duty of care starts when the luggage is handed to him or her and continues until it is retrieved. He or she must allow sufficient time at stops for passenger to claim their luggage, especially where this is stowed in lockers only accessible from outside the vehicle.

Lost property

Any person finding lost property on a bus is required by law to hand it to the driver or conductor, or, if this is not practical, to take it to the operator's lost property office (not to the police).

Drivers (or conductors) must search their vehicles for lost property at the end of each journey and be prepared to return this to anyone claiming it, *provided they can be satisfied as to ownership*. No fee (see below) is payable in this case. Otherwise they must hand it in for safe custody within 24 hours.

Operators have to keep a record of lost property. They can dispose of unclaimed lost property after a statutory period (usually three months but a shorter time for low value articles and perishable goods.) There is a schedule of charges which can be made for the return of lost property. Official documents such as passports must be returned to their issuing authority.

Standing passengers

The normal maximum number of standing passengers on a PSV is eight or ⅓ of the seating capacity of the bus (or lower saloon in the case of a double decker bus). However, smaller or larger numbers are frequently prescribed by certifying officers when a vehicle is given its Certificate of Initial Fitness or Certificate of Conformity and these limits must be observed by drivers. In addition an operator may decide, or agree with staff, to carry a lesser number of standing passengers. The maximum number of seated and standing passengers or the number which the operator is willing to carry must be shown on the inside of the vehicle in letters at least 25mm high, which must also be visible from outside the vehicle.

Standing passengers are not permitted:
(a) on a half deck vehicle
(b) on the top deck or stairs of a double decker bus
(c) on any part of the gangway forward of the driver
(d) on a PSV with 12 or fewer seats for passengers.

Seating capacity

On PSVs with nine or more passenger seats the number of seated passengers must not exceed the seating capacity of the vehicle as marked (see above).

However, in the case of children under 14 years of age, three seated children may count as two passengers. A child whose fourteenth birthday falls in a school term can be counted as a fourteen year old until the end of the school year in August.

ALCOHOL ON COACHES

It is an offence for alcohol to be carried (even if not consumed) on a PSV travelling to or from a "designated sporting event". The operator, hirer, or driver are all liable if they knowingly cause or permit this to happen. Police have powers to stop and search a PSV if they think the law is being infringed. Heavy penalties with maximum fines of up to £1000 and possible jail sentences can be imposed.

Designated sports grounds and sporting events The Sporting Events (Control of Alcohol) Act 1985 and its associated regulations make it an offence for alcohol to be carried on public service vehicles used principally for carrying passengers for the whole or part of a journey to or from a designated sports ground or sporting events.

The following is a list of such grounds and events.

England and Wales
1. The home grounds of all football clubs which are members of either the English or Welsh Football Associations.
2. Any other ground in England and Wales used by such clubs.
3. Wembley Stadium.
4. Any ground (not covered by 1-3 above) used for any international association football match in England and Wales.
5. Sheilfield Park, Berwick-upon-Tweed.

The designated sporting events concerned are:
  (a) association football matches where at least one of the participating teams is either a full or associate member of the Football League
  (b) international association football matches
  (c) association football matches in the European Cup; the Cup Winners' Cup; or the UEFA Cup
  (d) association football matches which come within the jurisdiction of the Scottish Football Association
  (e) association football matches which take place outside Great Britain where at least one of the participating teams either represents the English or Welsh Football Associations; or is a full or associate member of the Football League
  (f) association football matches outside Great Britain where at least one of the participating teams is a member of the English or Welsh Football Associations competing in the European Cup; the Cup Winners' Cup or the UEFA Cup.

Scotland

Annfield, Stirling
Bayview Park, Methil
Bellslea Park, Fraserburgh
Boghead Park, Dumbarton
Borough Briggs, Elgin
Brockville Park, Falkirk
Broomfield Park, Airdrie
Cappielow Park, Greenock
Celtic Park, Glasgow
Central Park, Cowdenbeath
Christie Park, Huntly
Claggan Park, Fort William
Cliftonhill Stadium, Coatbridge
Dens Park, Dundee
Douglas Park, Hamilton
Dudgeon Park, Brora
East End Park, Dunfermline
Easter Road Stadium, Edinburgh
Firhill Park, Glasgow
Fir Park, Motherwell
Firs Park, Falkirk
Gayfield Park, Arbroath
Glebe Park, Brechin
Grant Park, Lossiemouth
Grant Street Park, Inverness
Hampden Park, Glasgow
Ibrox Stadium, Glasgow
Kilbowie Park, Clydebank
Kingsmills Park, Inverness
Kynoch Park, Keith
Links Park, Montrose
MacKessack Park, Rothes
Meadowbank Stadium, Edinburgh
Mosset Park, Forres
Muirton Park, Perth
Murrayfield Stadium, Edinburgh
Ochilview Park, Stenhousemuir, Larbert
Palmerston Park, Dumfries
Pittodrie Stadium, Aberdeen

Princess Royal Park, Banff
Recreation Park, Alloa
Recreation Park, Peterhead
Rugby Park, Kilmarnock
St Mirren Park (Love Street), Paisley
Shawfield Stadium, Glasgow
Somerset Park, Ayr
Stair Park, Stranraer
Stark's Park, Kirkcaldy
Station Park, Forfar
Station Park, Nairn
Tannadice Park, Dundee
Telford Street Park, Inverness
Tynecastle Park, Edinburgh
Victoria Park, Buckie
Victoria Park, Dingwall

The classes of sporting events concerned are:
(a) association football matches in the Scottish Football League and the Highland Football League
(b) association football matches in the competition for the Scottish Association Cup; the Scottish Football League Cup; the Scottish Association Qualifying Cup (North); the European Cup; the European Cup Winners' Cup; or the UEFA Cup
(c) international football matches in Scotland
(d) association football matches (not covered by 1-3 above) which come within the jurisdication of the Scottish Football Association
(e) international Rugby Union football matches
(f) association football matches outside Great Britain in which one of the participating teams represents the Scottish Football Association; or is a member of either the Scottish Football League or the Highland Football League.

CLEANLINESS OF VEHICLES

Drivers should ensure that their vehicles are clean when in use. In particular vehicles should be washed whenever there is any danger of windows becoming too dirty for passengers to see out. It is especially important to ensure that the driver's windscreen is clean, the wipers and washers working and the screen wash bottle is topped up. The vehicle should be swept out and seats dusted and vacuumed regularly. Any torn upholstery, worn floor treads or projecting fastenings or trim which could injure a passenger or damage clothing should be reported. PSV examiners have been known to prohibit the use of a PSV where the above points have been neglected.

Finally, the visual appearance of the vehicle, both inside and out is very important, as is the appearance and manner of the driver — this is especially so where competition allows passengers a choice of services. Even where a choice is not available a dirty vehicle or offhand driver and/or conductor can result in passengers seeking other forms of transport which means the service being curtailed or eventually cancelled through lack of revenue.

FARES

On most local services and some longer distance services the drivers, unless they have conductors, are responsible for collecting fares and, usually, issuing tickets.

On some "flat fare" services passengers insert the correct fare into a glass fronted fare box and the driver simply checks this and operates a lever to desposit the coins in a sealed vault. On other services with graduated fares there are "Exact Fares Please" and "No Change Given" notices, so that drivers do not handle cash.

On the majority of services, however, drivers issue tickets and give change.

Some operators use tickets with pre-printed fare values, (eg the Ultimate Ticket Issuing Machine) but most systems now utilise ticket issuing machines which print the fare value onto blank ticket rolls, (eg the Setright Ticket Issuing Machine).

Revenue protection

The driver is responsible for protecting the operator's revenue. In some cases where a service subsidy has been won by tender the agreement may specify that the operator receives operating costs and the revenue goes to the tendering authority (Passenger Transport Executive or County Council). In this case the driver is responsible for a third party's revenue.

Inspections For the reasons given above the bus may be boarded by an inspector appointed by either the operator or the tendering authority, who will wish to be satisfied not only that passengers are paying the correct fare but also that the revenue is being properly accounted for.

In other words inspectors are legitimately looking for both passenger and driver fraud and if a driver obstructs an inspector in the execution of that duty it could have the effect of jeopardising the service subsidy agreement on which the driver's job may depend. The operator might also view such obstruction as misconduct.

Waybills The waybill is an essential accounting document which has to be reconciled with the cash taken by the driver. Depending on the ticketing system used, the driver may be asked to record the opening and closing serial numbers of pre-printed ticket stocks or the opening and closing cash register readings of the ticket machine.

Data Operators, and also tendering authorities who have to reimburse operators for concessionary fares taken and journeys made using off bus purchased tickets, need to collect data relating to passenger journeys.

Some operators ask drivers to record intermediate figures on their waybills at each terminus for this purpose, others rely on data sampling by their inspectors or specially appointed data collectors. Drivers should co-operate with these staff when they board their buses.

Fare tables

Fare tables usually show the single adult fare between fare stages. Additionally, child fares, OAP concessionary fares, and fares for dogs and parcels will be shown. In some cases a fare code is shown so that when there is a fares revision, new tables do not have to be created.

Typical Fare Table

Service 427

Oldham Town Centre
10 Clarksfield
20 10 Lees High Street
25 20 10 St John's Church
30 25 20 10 Waterhead
Concession (child 5–15 incl. and OAP, 12p)
Parcels and dogs half fare rounded up.

Typical Coded Fare Table

Service 427

Oldham Town Centre
A   Clarksfield
B   A   Lees High Street
C   B   A   St John's Church
D   C   B   A   Waterhead
Concession (Child 5–15 incl. and OAP = E)
Parcels and dogs half fare rounded up.
A = 10, B = 20, C = 25, D = 30, E = 12.

Tickets

It is essential that drivers ensure that passengers receive a ticket whenever they pay a fare. This is a receipt for the passenger and proves entitlement to travel. The issue of a ticket also supplies data to the operator and enables cash takings to be reconciled.

Off bus ticket sales Some operators sell season tickets and multi-journey tickets through outlets such as railway stations, post offices and newsagents. In many cases off bus sales are co-ordinated by PTEs and County Councils.

Multi-journey tickets are usually cancelled by cancellators on the vehicles, but in some cases it is the driver's responsibility to do so using a hand punch.

Most off bus sales are designed to be attractive to passengers by offering a discount on bulk purchases of journeys, unlimited travel for a period (week, month or year) on season tickets, interavailability on other operators' services and special off peak rates. They are also attractive to operators and drivers as cash is paid in advance and not on the bus and this speeds boarding times.

Drivers should familiarise themselves with the availability by time and route of these various pre-purchased tickets.

Stage numbers It is the drivers' responsibility to change stage numbers on ticket issuing and cancelling machines as the vehicles pass the various stages. Unless they do so inspectors cannot check their vehicles for over-riders.

Passes and permits Many passengers, such as pensioners and scholars (children too old to qualify for child fares but

still in full time education) are issued with permits by operators and local authorities indicating their entitlement to concessionary fares either:
(a) in general
(b) at specified times
(c) on certain journeys.

Other passengers, such as some disabled persons, employees of the company and in some areas, pensioners, may have free passes.

Drivers should be able to recognise the passes and permits which are valid on their buses, including those valid as a result of reciprical agreements with neighbouring authorities.

Electronic ticket issuing machines Many operators, including many minibus operators, are now using electronic ticket issuing machines, such as the Timtronic and Wayfarer.

These are speedy and simple to operate, reliable and fraudproof. They overcome many of the difficulties described above as follows.

1. They contain a ROM (read only memory) which is programmed to display the fare for any category of passenger between any two stages. The passenger states the destination and the driver enters the boarding/alighting points. The machine prints a correct value ticket.
2. They also contain a module on which details of every transaction are captured. (It may be necessary for this purpose for drivers to issue "nil fare taken" tickets to holders of free passes or season tickets). The module can be loaded by a driver and taken out when he or she leaves the vehicle. This not only obviates the need for completing a waybill, it also captures full passenger data for the operator. It can be read directly by a mini computer which is then able to analyse the day's takings by driver, route and vehicle.

It is the driver's responsibility to collect this machine (or module if the machine is mounted permanently in the vehicle) and to return these at the end of the duty. This is especially important in view of the high capital cost of the equipment.

Smartcards A relatively new system of fare collection, the smartcard is appearing in some operating areas. Passengers carry a credit card sized personal plastic card containing either a magnetic stripe or an embedded microchip. This can act either as an "electronic purse" on which is stored a pre-paid value (like a telephone card) which is "decremented" when wiped through the driver's electronic ticket machine (ETM), a travel entitlement or pass (eg for school children and some OAPs and disabled travellers with free passes), or a debit card on which information is exchanged between the microchip and ETM, sometimes with a contactless system (like the security gates in public libraries) capturing details of journeys taken and payments due. Drivers required to handle these systems will need to be trained to do so, although in most cases they work automatically with minimum driver involvement.

They are intended to speed boarding and improve travel data capture. The systems are in the main cashless, although some are designed to enable drivers to re-charge a smartcard to the value of cash offered.

ACCIDENTS AND INSURANCE

ACCIDENTS

One of the requirements outlined in the Highway Code (but never sufficiently appreciated by drivers) is the information that must be given in the event of an accident. The following procedure should be adopted:
1. Stop.
2. If any persons are injured seek assistance and send for an ambulance and the police.
3. Try to obtain witnesses.
4. Exchange particulars with the driver of any other vehicle involved, ie:
    (a) the name and address of the driver
    (b) the owner's name and address if the driver is not the owner
    (c) the registration number of the vehicle, its type and colour
    (d) where there is personal injury the name and address of the relevant insurance company.
5. Indicate:
    (a) the extent of any damage sustained
    (b) the time the accident occurred
    (c) where the accident occurred, ie:
        (i) the locality
        (ii) the names of streets and roads adjacent
        (iii) the position of the vehicles at the time of the accident
        (iv) the visibility at the time of the accident.
    (d) the cause of the accident (include any information on whether signals were given).
6. Provide a rough sketch to emphasise the general situation.

All drivers obviously hope that they will not be involved in an accident and are therefore content to leave any consideration of this procedure until one occurs.

It is accepted that drivers, experienced or otherwise, may become nervous and excited when involved in an accident. It is essential, however, that the correct information is obtained *at the time of the accident*. Once the involved parties have dispersed the true facts can never be recalled. This is particularly stressed so that drivers appreciate the important role of factual information in negotiation between insurance companies.

When involved in an accident drivers must not admit responsibility for the accident to the other party or to witnesses; they should leave this for the appropriate authorities to decide.

It should be noted, however, that the law requires a driver to stop and report any damage caused to property on or adjacent to the road or injury to certain animals as a result of an accident, to any person having reasonable grounds for requiring such information including details of insurance. If this cannot be done immediately then the police must be informed as soon as possible and in any case within 24 hours of the occurrence.

In the context of the above, *property* means any other vehicle(s), street furniture, ie traffic signs, bollards, etc, garden walls, fences, etc and *animal* means horses, asses, mules, cattle, sheep, pigs, goats or dogs.

Failure to stop or to report an accident is an offence and where reporting to the police is concerned this should be done as soon as possible; any delay (within the 24 hour period) may still bring prosecution if it is considered that the accident could have been reported earlier.

Accident forms

It is customary for insurance companies to issue accident forms and drivers should see that they carry and understand one of these, as it will serve as a useful guide for obtaining the required information.

Company procedures

In addition to the above legal requirements, many companies issue drivers with their own guidance on accident procedures.

The following is a summary of the more common procedures adopted.

The driver's first consideration should be for the safety and convenience of passengers. The driver must:
- ensure that any injured passengers or other road users receive medical attention as soon as possible
- if necessary, summon the emergency services or make sure that this is being done
- try to minimise the danger of any further accidents occurring as a result of the presence of his or her own and other

vehicles involved on the road, by arranging for a competent person to direct other road traffic
- arrange for a "change over vehicle" to be supplied so that uninjured passengers can continue their journey. (This may also be done by arranging for transfer of passengers onto a following service vehicle if there is room)
- if possible arrange for an inspector or supervisor to attend the scene of the accident to take statements from witnesses
- obtain the names and addresses of any witnesses to the accident, either bystanders or passengers.

Where the vehicle is in radio contact with the operator the above should not present any difficulty. In other cases the driver should try to find a telephone, reversing the charges if necessary.

INSURANCE

Compulsory cover

It is legally necessary to have insurance cover in accordance with the Traffic Acts and full third party insurance provides cover for personal injury and property damage sustained by third parties. Upon the issue of a third party policy, a certificate of insurance is also issued, which confirms that the cover conforms to the Acts. This certificate must be produced upon request from a police officer, or, if this is not possible, within seven days at any police station.

A third party insurance policy provides cover in respect of compensation for injury caused to another and also the cost of any emergency medical treatment resulting from an accident. Also included is legal liability for claims for damage to the property of third parties.

The Road Traffic Act 1988 requires that users of motor vehicles are covered against any liability which may occur in respect of death or personal injury to their passengers in the use of the vehicle on the road. All passengers must be covered and no "own risks" agreements are allowed.

If required, a third party policy can be extended to include risks of fire and theft of the insured vehicle. Should insurance be required to cover additional damage to the vehicle, it is necessary to take out a "comprehensive policy" which, apart from covering accidental damage, also embraces third party risks, fire and theft.

The Public Passenger Vehicles Act 1981 makes an operator absolutely liable for the safety of his passengers.

Production of insurance certificates Where a driver is required to produce a vehicle insurance certificate at a police station, there is no obligation for the driver to produce it "in person", the legal requirement is satisfied simply if the certificate is produced. The time limit for producing the document is "within seven days". However, if it cannot be produced within this period a defence is provided in the Road Traffic Act 1988 (s. 165) if it can be shown that it was produced at the police station as soon as possible, or, due to unforeseen circumstances, it was not reasonably practicable to produce the certificate before the day on which proceedings for non-production were started.

DRIVING OFFENCES

DRINK AND DRIVING

Under the provision of the Road Traffic Act 1988 it is an offence to drive, attempt to drive or be in charge of a motor vehicle, when having consumed alcohol in such quantity that the proportion of breath alcohol concentration exceeds the prescribed limit, ie 35mg of alcohol in 100ml of breath (which is equivalent to 80mg of alcohol in 100ml of blood or 107mg of alcohol in 100ml of urine).

Penalties prescribed are, on summary conviction, a fine not exceeding £5000, or imprisonment for up to six months, or both.

On conviction on indictment a fine or imprisonment of up to two years, or both, can be imposed (the maximum period of imprisonment on indictment for being in charge of a motor vehicle is one year). In addition, licence disqualification is usually imposed.

Breath tests and laboratory tests

A police constable in uniform can require a driver to take a breath test at the road side if:

(a) the officer has reasonable cause to suspect the driver of having alcohol in his or her body
(b) the officer has reasonable cause to suspect the driver of having committed a moving traffic offence
(c) the driver has been involved in an accident.

Failure to take the test, without reasonable cause, renders the driver liable to arrest and prosecution.

If a preliminary test indicates that the driver is over the limit he or she will be required to go to the police station and unless he or she goes voluntarily the driver can be arrested without a warrant.

At the police station the driver may be required to provide two samples of breath for analysis by an electronic breath testing machine (which gives an instant print out of breath alchohol concentrations) or a specimen of blood or urine for laboratory tests.

Failure, without reasonable cause, to provide a specimen of breath, blood or urine renders the driver liable to prosecution and the constable must warn when asking for a specimen.

A statement automatically produced by the breath testing machine, a certificate signed by the police constable that the statement relates to the breath specimen supplied and blood and urine specimens, shall be admissible as evidence in a prosecution.

A blood specimen may only be taken by a medical practitioner and with the driver's consent.

Of any two breath specimens provided the lower must be used, except if the lower specimen shows no more than 50 microgrammes of alcohol in 100ml of breath the driver has the right to replace the breath test with a blood or urine test.

The driver may be detained at the police station until the breath test indicates that the alcohol level is below the prescribed limit.

There is a statutory defence against being "in charge" of a motor vehicle if a driver can prove that, at the time, circumstances were such that there was no likelihood of him or her driving whilst exceeding the prescribed limits or whilst unfit through drugs.

Where there has been an accident involving injury to a third party, the police have the power to enter any place where a drink/drive suspect may be, using force if necessary, both to breathalyse and to arrest that person.

DISQUALIFICATION

There are offences for which:
  (a) endorsement is compulsory unless there are special reasons
  (b) courts have discretionary powers to disqualify
  (c) if **12** penalty points are accumulated over three years, disqualification will result for at least six months. Once a period of disqualification has been imposed the existing points incurred under the totting-up procedure will be removed from the licence issued to the driver.

Where more than one offence is committed on the same occasion separate points may be incurred for separate offences.

The three year period is a rolling term, ie it is measured on each occasion from the date the latest offence was committed.

When disqualification is imposed after the total number of points have been awarded the period of disqualification will be:

- *six months*, if there has been no previous disqualification within the three years
- *one year*, if there has been one previous disqualification within the three years
- *two years*, if there has been more than one disqualification within the three years.

Disqualification can still be imposed for a single offence if it is considered to be serious enough and the liability to obligatory disqualification is retained for drinking and driving offences. (Drivers disqualified on conviction for drunken driving are subject to a minimum ban of one year for a first offence and three years for a second conviction for drunken driving within 10 years.)

OFFENCES FOR WHICH PENALTY POINTS ARE AWARDED

Courts disqualifying a driver for any of the specified offences below may order him or her to undergo another driving test before reissuing the licence.

Offence	No. of points
Contravention of temporary prohibition or restriction	3–6*
Use of special road contrary to scheme or regulations	3–6*
Contravention of pedestrian crossing regulations	3
Not stopping at school crossing	3
Contravention of order relating to street playground	2
Exceeding speed limit	3–6*
Causing death by dangerous driving	(a)
Dangerous driving	(a)
Careless and inconsiderate driving	3–9
Causing death by careless driving when under the influence of drink or drugs	(a)
Driving or attempting to drive when unfit to drive through drink or drugs	(a)

* 3 if fixed penalty

(a) 3–11 points if under exceptional circumstances disqualification is not imposed

Offence	No. of points
Being in charge of a vehicle when unfit to drive through drink or drugs	10
Being in charge of a mechanically propelled vehicle with excess alcohol in body	10
Failing to provide a specimen for breath test	4
Failing to provide specimen for analysis or laboratory test	(a)(b)
Motor racing and speed trials on public ways	(a)
Leaving vehicles in dangerous positions	3
Failing to comply with traffic directions	3
Failing to comply with traffic signs	3
Using vehicle in dangerous condition, etc	3
Breach of requirements as to brakes, steering gear or tyres	3
Driving otherwise than in accordance with a licence	3–6
Driving with defective eyesight, or refusing an eyesight test	3
Driving after making false declaration as to physical fitness	3–6
Failing to comply with conditions attached to a provisional or full licence	2
Driving following the failure to notify onset of, or deterioration in, relevant or prospective disability	3–6
Driving after refusal of licence or revocation	3–6
Driving while disqualified—	
where offender was disqualified as under age	2
where offender was disqualified by order of court	7
Using motor vehicle without insurance	6–8
Failing to stop after accident and give particulars or report accident	5–10
Failure of keeper of vehicle and others to give police information as to identity of driver, etc in the case of certain offences	3
Manslaughter or, in Scotland, culpable homicide	(a)

(a) 3–11 points if under exceptional circumstances disqualification is not imposed
(b) 10 points, depending on circumstances, if disqualification is not imposed.

OFFENCES FOR WHICH FINES ARE IMPOSED

Fines are imposed for the following offences:
- obstructing a certifying officer or vehicle examiner from inspecting a PSV, or from entering premises where such vehicles are kept, for the purpose of inspection
- driving a PSV or causing or permitting the vehicle to be driven, in contravention of a prohibition
- contravention of conditions attached to a PSV operator's licence
- failure to exhibit a PSV operator's disc on the vehicle
- failure to inform Traffic Commissioners of any relevant convictions when applying for, or whilst holding an operator's licence or failure to inform Traffic Commissioners of material change in operating conditions of the holder of the operator's licence
- contravention of regulations providing for the control of number of passengers in public service vehicles
- failure to give notice to Traffic Commissioners relating to failure in, damage to or alteration of a public service vehicle or other information relating to the vehicles in the operator's possession
- providing false information about PSVs in licence holder's possession
- making false statements in order to obtain operator's licence, PSV driver's licence or variations to such licences, Certificates of Initial Fitness, type approval certificates, operator's discs or certificate of professional competence
- contravention of regulations made under the Public Passenger Vehicles Act 1981
- failure to give identity of driver of PSV in certain cases
- driving a PSV without a PSV driver's licence or PCV entitlement or employing a driver without such a licence to drive a PSV
- contravention of regulations as to conduct of drivers, conductors or inspectors of PSVs
- failing to produce driver's licence for endorsement
- contravention of regulations as to conduct of passengers in PSVs
- failure of persons carrying on the business of operating PSVs to keep accounts and records and to make financial and statistical returns

- forging and misusing documents appertaining to certificates of initial fitness, operator's licences and discs, PSV drivers' licences or PCV entitlement, type approval certificates, certificate of professional competence, a certifying officer or PSV examiner authorisation*
- contravention of prohibition or restrictions of vehicles using roads of certain classes
- contravention of provisions as to use of special road
- contravention of weight limits on bridges
- contravention of pedestrian crossing regulations
- failing to stop at school crossings
- causing death by dangerous driving†
- dangerous driving*
- careless and inconsiderate driving
- driving or attempting to drive when under the influence of drink or drugs*
- driving or attempting to drive with excess alcohol in breath, blood or urine*
- being in charge of a motor vehicle when unfit to drive through drink or drugs*
- being in charge of a motor vehicle with excess alcohol in breath, blood or urine*
- failing to provide a specimen for analysis or laboratory test:
  (a) where it was required for ascertaining ability to drive or proportion of alcohol at time the person was driving or attempting to drive*
  (b) in any other case*
- failing to submit to a breath test
- speeding
- racing on the highway
- failing to heed traffic directions
- leaving vehicle in a dangerous position
- failing to stop after an accident or report the accident
- obstructing a vehicle from being inspected after an accident
- tampering with vehicles
- driving or riding in a motor vehicle and not wearing a seat belt
- driving a motor vehicle with a child in the front not wearing a seat belt
- driving motor vehicle elsewhere than on roads
- prohibition of parking heavy commercial vehicles on verges and footways

- contravention of Construction and Use Regulations by using or causing or permitting the use of a vehicle adapted to carry more than eight passengers in that it is likely to cause danger:
  (a) by its general condition; the number of passengers being carried; or the weight, distribution, packing or adjustment of the load; the condition of the vehicle's brakes, steering-gear, tyres, or any description of weight; or by its unsuitability
  (b) by the vehicle having an insecure load
  (c) in other cases
- using a vehicle without test certificate:
  (a) when adapted to carry more than eight passengers
  (b) in any other case
- using a vehicle that has been altered but not notified to the authorities
- using a vehicle without certificate showing the type approval requirements applicable to it
- obstructing an examiner from testing vehicle on the road
- failure of owner of defective vehicle to give certificate
- failure of driver of vehicle on roadside test to give particulars of the owner
- obstructing further testing of vehicle after a reasonable time following the issue of a defect certificate
- selling faulty vehicles or trailers or altering them to make them unroadworthy
- selling vehicle or vehicle part without required certificate showing type approval requirements applicable to it
- drawing more than permitted number of trailers
- allowing vehicle to be on the road without proper lighting
- driving without a licence or employing a person to drive without appropriate entitlement
- failure to comply with the conditions of a provisional licence or full licence treated as a provisional licence
- holding driving licence when particulars are incorrect
- driving with defective eyesight
- refusing to submit to eyesight test
- obtaining a driving licence when disqualified
- driving when disqualified*
- failing to produce licence for endorsement and/or disqualification, etc
- applying for or obtaining a licence without disclosing current endorsements

- failing to produce licence to court making order for interim disqualification to committal for sentence, etc
- failing to produce to court Northern Ireland driving licence
- failing to give or provide evidence of date of birth or sex
- unregistered and unlicensed persons giving driving instructions for payment
- using motor vehicle without third party insurance
- failing to surrender insurance certificate to insurer on cancellation or to advise its loss or destruction
- failing to give information or making false statements on insurance claims
- failing to stop when required by a constable
- failing to produce driving licence to a police constable
- giving false particulars when stopped for careless or dangerous driving
- failure of driver involved in an accident, where injury to a person occurs, to produce evidence of insurance or report accident
- failure of vehicle owner to supply the police with information to verify the requirements of compulsory insurance
- forgery of licences, test certificates, insurance certificates, etc
- producing false evidence or making false declarations in order to obtain excise licence for vehicle requiring test certificate
- making false statements in connection with the remedying of vehicle defects found on roadside tests
- failure to notify the driving licence authorities of onset of, deterioration in, relevant or prospective disability
- making false statements or withholding information to obtain insurance certificates, etc
- issuing false insurance certificates, test certificates, etc
- failure to attend inquiry, give evidence or produce documents
- failing to attend inquiry when so ordered
- failing to attend or produce documents before a Transport Tribunal
- failing to comply with an operator's licence
- failing to keep records as to hours of work, etc
- failing to preserve records
- failing to produce records
- using a vehicle without an excise licence
- failure to exhibit an excise licence

- failure to observe the automatic half-barrier level crossing regulations

† imprisonment
* fine and/or imprisonment.

REMOVAL OF DISQUALIFICATION

A person who has been disqualified may apply to the clerk of the court which imposed the disqualification for the removal of the disqualification under the following conditions:
  (a) if the disqualification is for less than four years, when two years from the date on which it was imposed have expired
  (b) if the disqualification is for less than 10 years but not less than four years, when half the period of disqualification has expired
  (c) in any other case, when five years have expired from the date of disqualification.

If the first removal application is refused, others can be made at three monthly intervals.

If disqualification is for two years or less application for the removal of the disqualification cannot be made. However, application to the quarter sessions for a reduction of the period can be made within 14 days of conviction and disqualification.

Courts disqualifying a driver from driving for any of the offences outlined in the above-mentioned schedules may order another driving test to be taken and passed prior to the reissue of the licence. A driving test cannot be ordered for any other road traffic offence.

If prosecuted for any of the offences listed, the driver must:
  (a) submit his or her driving licence to the clerk of the court not later than the day before the hearing or
  (b) post the licence to the court to be received not later than the day of the hearing or
  (c) take the licence to the hearing.

REMOVAL OF ENDORSEMENTS

Endorsements are not removed from a driving licence until four years after conviction. For drinking and other driving offences the endorsements remain for 11 years.

DUAL LIABILITY

Both the driver or owner-driver and the employer are liable if any of the under-mentioned offences is committed:
- contravention of an order relating to street playgrounds
- contravention of construction and use regulations:
  (a) in a manner likely to cause danger (vehicle overweight, insecure load, etc)
  (b) by breach of requirements as to brakes, steering gear, tyres
  (c) by driving whilst unqualified and employing and allowing a person who does not hold a licence to drive the type of motor vehicle in question
  (d) by the use of a motor vehicle uninsured or unsecured against third party risks.

An employer who permits or causes the vehicle to be used can also be prosecuted. Under the Road Traffic Act 1988, a defence can be made if the employer can prove that he or she did not know that the offence had been committed.

USE OF VEHICLES ON THE ROAD

SPEED LIMITS

Speed limits are governed by the Road Traffic Regulation Act 1984 and apply to roads and vehicles. Where these are different, the lower of the two applies.

General speed limits must be observed by all vehicles on the specific stretch of road to which the limit applies.

The maximum permitted speed on dual carriageways and motorways in Great Britain is 70mph and on single carriageway roads 60mph unless lower speed limits are in force for that road, or the vehicle is in a class which restricts it to a lower limit (see below).

Lower speed limits, usually 30mph, but lesser statutory limits can be imposed, apply to all vehicles on *restricted roads* which either have street lights at intervals of not more than 200 yards or are designated as restricted and have "repeater" speed limit signs erected. Where the 30mph limit has been increased or decreased on a specific restricted road this is indicated by appropriate traffic signs.

Mandatory speed limits (which must not be exceeded) at roadworks on motorways are shown as black figures on a white ground enclosed in a red circle, ie the same signs as used on restricted roads to denote speed limits.

Particular Speed Limits For Certain Classes of Vehicle

Class of vehicle	Motor-ways	Dual Carriageways (other than motorways)	Other Roads
1. A passenger vehicle with an unladen weight exceeding 3.05 tonnes **or** adapted to carry more than eight passengers:			
(i) not exceeding 12m in overall length	70	60*	50*
(ii) exceeding 12m in overall length (articulated vehicle)	60†	60*	50*
2. Dual-purpose vehicle if adapted to carry more than eight passengers	70	60*	50*

Class of vehicle	Motor-ways	Dual Carriageways (other than motorways)	Other Roads
3. A passenger vehicle, car-derived van or dual-purpose vehicle drawing one trailer	60	60*	50*

† articulated buses are not allowed to use the outside lane of motorways which have three or more lanes.
* provided the dual carriageway or other road is not subject to a lower limit.

Exemptions from speed limits

Vehicles being used for fire brigade, ambulance or police purposes are exempt from speed limits if such limits are likely to hinder the use of the vehicle for the purpose for which it is being used on that occasion.

Coach speeds driving standards

The Bus and Coach Council has drawn up a Code of Conduct on coach speeds and driving standards which has been approved by the Department of Transport.

The code is reproduced in full below and its contents should be carefully noted by drivers of coaches and buses, especially those engaged in long distance operations when driving to the maximum speeds allowed.

CODE OF CONDUCT

Background

1. In accordance with the agreement reached between the Bus and Coach Council and the Minister of State for Transport, this voluntary Code of Conduct has been produced with the objective of securing compliance by coaches with the vehicle speed limits on motorways or derestricted dual carriageways and of securing the driving standards recommended in the Highway Code.
2. Unless there are lower speed limits for all traffic on certain stretches of road, the current speed limits for coaches are:

Motorways	70 miles per hour*
Dual carriageways	60 miles per hour
Other roads	50 miles per hour

* 60 miles per hour for articulated vehicles.

3. This Code of Conduct has been discussed with the Department of Transport and has received its approval. The Bus and Coach Council expects all its members to comply with the Code and non-members are also strongly recommended to comply with it.
4. Under the Public Passenger Vehicles Act 1981, the Traffic Commissioners are required, when considering applications for operators' licences, to be satisfied that there will be adequate arrangements for securing compliance by the operator with the requirements of the law relating to the driving and operation of that operator's vehicles. In considering future applications, the Traffic Commissioners may well wish to be satisfied that operators are taking reasonable steps to ensure compliance with speed limits and satisfactory standards of driver behaviour.

Scope of code
5. This Code of Conduct covers the use of all buses and coaches on motorways or derestricted dual carriageways on any type of operation, except when the vehicle is not capable of exceeding the relevant speed limit, or is used on regular local or express services covering less than 10 continuous miles on such roads.

Provisions of code
6. All coaches operating under this Code will be fitted with calibrated and sealed tachographs which comply with the two-yearly calibration check and six-yearly recalibration legal requirements. Those coaches whose use would fall within the scope of the Code and which are not already fitted with tachographs should be fitted with the necessary equipment as soon as possible.
7. Although calibrated and sealed tachographs are not required by law for operations on regular services, such tachographs and the appropriate discs should be used on these operations, as well as other operations, in order to record speed.
8. Where, due to unforeseen difficulties such as those caused by bad weather, accidents or emergencies, it may from time to time be necessary for the holder of the operators' licence to use a coach which is not equipped with a

calibrated and sealed tachograph (but which is capable of exceeding the relevant speed limit) he should ensure that a specific record is kept of each instance, including the reason for not complying with the Code on regular services.

9. In addition to any checks of tachograph discs for compliance with drivers' hours regulations, tachograph discs should be monitored to determine whether or not the 70 miles per hour speed limit on motorways has been exceeded and every effort should be made in this monitoring to ensure that the 60 miles per hour limit on derestricted dual carriageways is adhered to.

10. Every operator should ensure that his staff are instructed to monitor tachograph discs in accordance with paragraph 9 and report to him any breaches of speed limits on motorways and derestricted dual carriageways which are disclosed.

11. It will then be the responsibility of the holder of the operator's licence to ensure that appropriate action, aimed at preventing further infringements, is promptly taken.

12. In scheduling any work which includes operation on motorways or derestricted dual carriageways, whether regular or non-regular, realistic running times should be allowed by the operator, having due regard to the likely effect of such established factors as long term roadworks, seasonal or peak-period congestion and the like. Where the time allowed proves to be inadequate, the appropriate speed limits must still be observed by drivers.

13. The holder of an operator's licence should take all reasonable steps to ensure that his drivers are fully aware of the laws concerning tachographs and their use and of speed limits and the necessity of complying with them. This requirement includes part time drivers and other staff driving occasionally.

14. The holder of the operator's licence should also ensure that his drivers are aware of the provisions of the Highway Code and particularly those relating to driving on motorways and dual carriageways, regarding safe driving and that appropriate action is taken where breaches of the Highway Code are brought to his attention.

15. Staff involved in the scheduling or operation of coaches under this Code should receive suitable instruction and

particularly those involved in the scheduling of services or the preparation of itineraries for tours, excursions or private hires, or the monitoring of tachograph discs.

USE OF CAR TELEPHONES AND/OR MICROPHONES

A telephone handset should not be used by a driver whilst the vehicle is in motion, except in an emergency. Neither should a vehicle be stopped on the hard shoulder of a motorway for the driver to make or receive a call no matter how urgent.

Neckslung or clipped-on microphones may be used provided the attention of the driver is not likely to be distracted during use.

DRIVING ON MOTORWAYS

Motorways are designed for the purpose of permitting motor vehicles to travel at speed with safety, provided that the rules and regulations laid down are strictly obeyed.

Maximum safety will not be assured unless drivers using motorways are experienced in road procedure and lane drill.

Drivers must also be adept in handling vehicles at speed under prevailing conditions, which include "night driving". Treat the following as a code of practice.
1. Observation drill.
2. Mirror drill.
3. Direction indicator drill.
4. Lights drill.

Rules
A driver must not:
  (a) drive anywhere but on the carriageway
  (b) stop on the carriageway
  (c) reverse on the carriageway
  (d) stop on the central reservation
  (e) stop on verges or hard shoulder, except in case of breakdown, accident or other emergency
  (f) walk on the carriageway or central reservation, except in an emergency

(g) make a "U-turn"
(h) use the *third lane* when driving an articulated passenger vehicle on a three (or more) lane motorway
(i) disobey remote control signals, such as warning signals — Lane Closed, Maximum Advised Speed, and all other flashing amber light signals
(j) leave the motorway by an entry road.

Conduct on motorways

1. When joining a motorway (other than at its start) the approach will be from a road on the left (slip road). Give way to traffic already on the motorway, watch for a safe gap in the traffic inside lane, then accelerate so that the vehicle is travelling at roughly the same speed as the traffic on it.
2. Drive at a steady speed within the limits of the vehicle. On wet or icy roads, or in fog keep the speed down.
3. Driving for long distances can cause drowsiness. To help prevent this make sure there is a flow of fresh air in the vehicle, suck sweets or turn off at an exit or, if nearby, pull into a service area.
4. Exercise caution and drive well within the limits.
5. Know the braking and stopping distances (see *Highway Code*).
6. Extend courtesy to other road users.
7. Do not "hog" the second or centre lanes.

Motorway signals

Signals are used on many stretches of motorway and these are usually positioned at two mile intervals on the central reservation and apply to all lanes. On some very busy stretches overhead gantry signals are used.

When the road ahead is clear the signals are blank but in dangerous conditions amber lights flash and the central panel of the signal will indicate either in figures (which means a temporary speed limit) or symbols (arrows, etc) that a change of lane is necessary, or that the driver must leave the motorway at the next exit, due to an obstruction ahead.

The signals on overhead gantries, which are positioned over each lane, may also show a flashing red light which means that the vehicle must not **continue beyond the signal in that lane**. Similarly, if red lights flash on a slip road it must not be entered.

All signals should be obeyed since they are there to warn against danger ahead even though it may not be visible.

Driving in fog on motorways
Before starting any journey in foggy conditions drivers should:
- (a) check that all lights and reflectors are clean and that lights and indicators are working properly
- (b) clean the windscreen and windows and keep them clean by using wipers, windscreen washer and demister.

1. A proper speed, safe separation distance and the maintaining of a safe level of speed are essential.
2. There is an advisory speed of 30mph for driving in fog.
3. Fog affects judgement of speed and drivers can easily find themselves speeding up without realising it.
4. Fog makes tail-lights seem further away than they really are.
5. Drivers should know the stopping distances of their vehicles and allow for these.
6. Drivers should use *headlights* or front *fog lights* (if fitted) and *rear fog lights*.

Prohibitions
Among the vehicles that may *not* use motorways are:
- vehicles driven by learner drivers
- pedestrian-controlled vehicles
- animal-drawn vehicles
- agricultural tractors, etc taxed at reduced rate
- engineering plant
- vehicles normally subject to 20mph speed limit.

Breakdowns
1. If the vehicle breaks down get it on to the hard shoulder, if possible, and leave sufficient room for working on the offside.
2. If help is needed, use the emergency telephone giving an appropriate description of the vehicle and position. From the information in the documents carried give details of equipment, components or tyres, etc, which may assist the police in correctly advising the breakdown services of the requirements.

3. The driver should not wander away from the vehicle as the emergency control cannot call back, so if there is any undue delay a further call should be made to the emergency services.

Condition of vehicles

Vehicle roadworthiness is essential for long journeys and when travelling at speed.

Particular efficiency is required on brakes, steering, batteries and lights, tyres and direction indicators.

Make sure that the following are checked and are in good order, as so many breakdowns and accidents are caused by the neglect of them:
- oil and water levels
- fuel
- fan belt (and spare)
- brakes
- tyres (condition and inflation pressures), spare wheel and jack
- driving mirrors, windscreen wipers and washers
- lights and reflectors
- steering.

PEDESTRIAN CROSSINGS AND BUS LANES

Zebra crossings

Zebra crossings consist of rows of alternate black and white stripes between two rows of round or square-headed metal studs placed across the road and marked by a yellow globe on a post containing a flashing light (Belisha beacon). In certain circumstances a constant light may be used.

On either the approach side or both sides of the zebra crossing (depending on local requirements), there is a "zebra controlled area" consisting of two or more white broken zigzag lines, starting from short lines across the road and approaching the crossing, finishing at a dotted line, the give way line, 1m before reaching the row of metal studs edging the actual zebra crossing.

In the zebra controlled area *overtaking is prohibited and vehicles must stop at the give way line.*

Stopping in the controlled area or on the crossing is also prohibited except to allow pedestrians to cross, or in circumstances beyond the driver's control.

Pedestrians must be given the right of way if they are already on a crossing before a vehicle reaches it. On roads divided by a central reservation or a street refuge (island), each half of the road is treated as a separate crossing.

Pelican crossings

Pelican crossings are controlled by lights and are operated by pedestrians. The difference between conventional three-light signals and the pelican signals is the flashing amber signal which appears immediately after the red as opposed to the red/amber signal. Pedestrians continue to have precedence on a crossing when the amber light is flashing but if no pedestrians are crossing vehicles may proceed.

Zebra crossing style zig-zag markings are now being applied to pelican crossings and in the controlled area drivers are prohibited from overtaking a vehicle in front of them. Also they may not park or stop in the controlled area unless required to do so at the give way line.

Bus lanes

Bus lanes on general purpose roads are reserved for public service vehicles only and it is an offence for other vehicles to enter these lanes when they are in operation (usually during peak hours). The lanes are clearly marked with special signs indicating times of operation.

Red Routes

A pilot scheme for a priority route network is now operating in London. Known as the "Red Route" double red lines marked on roads mean that vehicles are prohibited from stopping at any time and on roads painted with single red lines stopping for loading and unloading is only permitted *outside* working hours.

The "red route" scheme is due to be expanded in the capital in the near future. Fixed penalties for illegal parking will be higher than on other routes.

De-criminalisation of parking offences in London

Part II of the Road Traffic Act 1991 provides that contraventions of order relating to designated parking places in

London will no longer be a criminal offence and provision is made for authorities (Metropolitan Boroughs) to appoint their own parking attendants, "clamp" illegally parked vehicles and to impose penalties (recoverable as civil debts). The Joint Committee of London Authorities may appoint Parking Adjudicators to conduct a hearing in disputed cases.

PARKING RESTRICTIONS

1. It is an offence to leave a vehicle unattended without stopping the engine and securely applying the handbrake.
2. A vehicle and trailer must not be left on the road in such a position as to cause an obstruction.
3. A trailer must not be left on a road detached from the towing vehicle unless the brake is set on at least one wheel or it is secured by a chain, chock or other efficient device to prevent the wheel from moving.
4. Vehicles must not be parked opposite another vehicle or a road island.
5. Vehicles must not be parked in a dangerous position, ie on a bridge, on a bend, within the studs of a pedestrian crossing, double white lines and clearways.

The following observations apply mainly to tour coaches and not to drivers of local services where stopping for passengers to alight or board is mainly at recognised bus stops.

Loading and unloading hours

These are shown by short yellow lines one foot long painted on the kerb and indicate the following:

(a) *single marks* at *intervals* — loading ban at peak hours (am and pm marked on lamp-post)
(b) *double marks* at *intervals* — loading ban throughout the day, eg 08.00 to 18.30 pm
(c) *treble marks* at *intervals* — loading bans for more than the working day, eg 08.00 to midnight.

No waiting and parking

These restrictions are indicated by yellow lines painted in the gutter and they do not prevent the picking up and setting down of passengers. Indeed, many local Acts and Orders permit vehicles to stand in "No waiting" streets for this specific purpose and this is especially so in the case of the growing "hail and ride" urban minibus services.

There are three types of yellow lines:
(a) the dotted line which indicates "no waiting" for part of the day
(b) the solid yellow line which indicates "no waiting" for the normal working day
(c) the double yellow line which indicates "no waiting" for more than the working day.

Like the kerb signs, the times of these bans will be shown on the lamp-post signs.

Notes:
1. Drivers may only stop to pick up and set down in a "no waiting" street and not for any other purpose.
2. A police officer has the right to move drivers on.

Breakdown and removal of vehicles
1. If a vehicle breaks down in a prohibited street and must be left in order to obtain assistance, the police or traffic wardens should be notified.
2. The police are empowered to remove any vehicle which is causing an obstruction, contravening waiting restrictions or left in a dangerous position.

Parking meters
Parking meters are included with the kerb marking signs which are displayed on discs to indicate the "controlled zone".

Double parking beside parking bays, etc which are already occupied is prohibited.

Traffic wardens
Traffic wardens are empowered to enforce the following legal requirements:
(a) compulsory lights or reflectors
(b) waiting and parking restrictions by use of the fixed penalty system.

Fixed penalty system
Fixed fines can be imposed without the case being heard in court. This system operates in towns and cities throughout the country.

Under this system tickets may be issued by traffic wardens for offences as outlined above and also for: parking at night without obligatory lights or reflectors; not showing a current excise licence; making "U" turns in prohibited places; lighting offences committed by moving vehicles; banned right turns and driving the wrong way in a one-way street.

The Road Traffic (Offenders) Act 1988 provides for registered owners of motor vehicles to carry the ultimate responsibility for the payment of certain *fixed penalty* and *excess* parking charges when these have not been settled within the time allowed, ie 28 days. The liabilities relate to fixed penalties for the following:

(a) parking a vehicle on a road during the hours of darkness without lights or reflectors required by law
(b) contravention of waiting, parking, loading and unloading restrictions
(c) non-payment of a parking meter charge
(d) keeping a vehicle on a public road without a current licence.

Owner liability also extends to excess charges.

Exceptions to these requirements are:

(a) the registered owner shall not be deemed to be the driver if it is proved that at the relevant time the vehicle was in the possession of some other person without the owner's consent
(b) in the case of hired vehicles (hired for less than six months) the payment of the relevant charges rests with the hirer and not the registered owner.

Whilst the ultimate responsibility for the settlement of unpaid charges rests with the owner, this in no way absolves the actual driver.

The Transport Act 1988 extended the fixed penalty system to cover other traffic offences, including motorway regulations, speeding, failing to comply with traffic directions and various vehicle defect offences, etc and the complete list is as follows:

1. Leaving a vehicle parked at night without lights or reflectors
2. Waiting, parking, loading or unloading
3. Controlled parking zone regulations
4. Failure to display a current excise licence disc
5. Making "U" turns in unauthorised places
6. Lighting offences by moving vehicles
7. Banned right turns and driving the wrong way in a one-way street

8. Contravening a traffic regulation order
9. Breach of experimental traffic order
10. Breach of experimental traffic scheme regulation in Greater London
11. Using a vehicle in contravention of a temporary prohibition or restriction of traffic on a road, ie where a road is being repaired, etc
12. Contravening motorway traffic regulations
13. Driving a vehicle in contravention of order prohibiting or restricting driving vehicles on certain classes of roads
14. Breach of pedestrian crossing regulations*
15. Contravention of a street playground order*
16. Breach of a parking place order on a road
17. Breach of a provision of a parking place designation order and other offences committed in relation to it, except failing to pay an excess charge
18. Contravening a parking place designation order
19. Breach of a provision of a parking place designation order
20. Contravention of minimum speed limits
21. Speeding†
22. Driving or keeping a vehicle without displaying registration mark or hackney carriage sign
23. Driving or keeping a vehicle with registration mark or hackney carriage sign obscured
24. Failure to comply with traffic directions or signs
25. Leaving vehicle in a dangerous position
26. Failing to wear a seat-belt
27. Breach of restriction on carrying children in the front of vehicles
28. Breach of restriction on carrying children in the rear of vehicles
29. Driving a vehicle elsewhere than on the road
30. Parking a vehicle on the path or verge
31. Breach of construction and use regulations*
32. Contravention of lighting restrictions on vehicles
33. Driving without a licence*
34. Breach of provisional licence conditions†
35. Failure to stop when required by constable in uniform
36. Obstruction of highway with vehicle

---

* endorsement is obligatory in certain circumstances.
† endorsement is obligatory.

For most of these offences only police officers will issue fixed penalty tickets; traffic wardens will continue to deal mainly with parking offences.

Police officers will still be able to warn drivers. In appropriate cases a police officer will issue a fixed penalty ticket or, in more serious cases, prosecute in the normal way. Once a police officer has issued a fixed penalty ticket the driver will have 28 days (or as specified in the notice) to pay. The driver still has the option to contest the offence in court and this is explained clearly on the fixed penalty notice. If the driver does not take either course within 28 days the penalty will be increased by 50% and enforced by the courts as an unpaid fine. Thus a £20 (£30 in London) non-endorsable fixed penalty becomes a £30 (£45) fine and the £40 (licence endorsable) penalty rises to £60.

The fixed penalty tickets for the less serious non-endorsable offences are usually white.

The endorsable tickets are yellow and attract the higher penalty of £40. Where a police officer has decided to issue a fixed penalty ticket for an endorsable offence the driver's licence will be required so that the existing number of penalty points can be checked. A ticket will be issued and the driver asked to surrender the licence in return for a receipt which will be valid for two months. If the penalty points for the present offence added to those which may already be on the licence total 12 or more — the level for disqualification — the driver will not be issued with a fixed penalty notice but will be reported for prosecution. A driver who is not carrying a licence will be required to take it to the police station of his or her choice within seven days. If a driver is stopped for an endorsable offence it will therefore be much more convenient if he or she is carrying his or her driving licence.

Penalty points for traffic offences are given on page 124.

Parking on the road at night without lights

The Road Vehicles Lighting Regulations 1984 allow vehicles to be parked on the road at night without lights in the following circumstances.

Motor cars, motorcycles and passenger vehicles adapted to carry not more than *eight* passengers provided that:
  (a) the road is subject to a 30mph speed limit, or less
  (b) no part of the vehicle is within 10m of a road junction

(c) the vehicle is parked close to the kerb and parallel to it and, except in the case of one-way streets, has its nearside to the kerb.

On all other roads and in other circumstances the obligatory side and rear lights must be switched on.

Passenger vehicles adapted to carry *nine or more* passengers excluding the driver, goods vehicles *exceeding* 1525kg unladen weight and any vehicle to which a trailer is attached, must keep their lights (side lamps) on when parked on the road at night.

When lights are required on a parked vehicle two white lights must be shown at the front and two red lights to the rear.

It is *illegal* to use either a single parking light or a device which switches on only the offside front and rear lamps.